BIG FREEDIA

GOD SAVE THE QUEEN DIVA!

BIG FREEDIA

GOD SAVE THE QUEEN DIVA!

BIG FREEDIA

WITH NICOLE BALIN

GALLERY BOOKS

NEW YORK   LONDON   TORONTO   SYDNEY   NEW DELHI

G

Gallery Books
An Imprint of Simon & Schuster, Inc.
1230 Avenue of the Americas
New York, NY 10020

All photos courtesy of the author's collection, except: family portrait of author, Crystal, Adam, and their mother: Olan Mills Photography, 1992/courtesy of author's collection; photo of author at Echoplex, courtesy of Koury Angelo; photo of author's mother's funeral cortege, courtesy of Beto Lopez; photo of Steph, the author, and Tootie, courtesy of and copyright Fuse, LLC © 2014.

Bounce primer designs by Ian O'Phelan

First Gallery Books hardcover edition July 2015

For information about special discounts for bulk purchases,
please contact Simon & Schuster Special Sales at 1-866-506-1949
or business@simonandschuster.com.

The Simon & Schuster Speakers Bureau can bring authors to your live event.
For more information or to book an event contact the Simon & Schuster Speakers Bureau at 1-866-248-3049 or visit our website at www.simonspeakers.com.

Interior design by Davina Mock-Maniscalco
Cover design by John Vairo Jr.
Photography by Koury Angelo Photography

Manufactured in the United States of America

10 9 8 7 6 5 4 3 2 1

Library of Congress Cataloging-in-Publication Data

Big Freedia, author.
  Big Freedia : God save the queen diva! / by Big Freedia and Nicole Balin.
—First Gallery Books hardcover edition.
    pages cm
1. Big Freedia. 2. Rap musicians—United States—Biography. 3. Television personalities—United States—Biography. I. Balin, Nicole, author. II. Title.
ML420.B547A3 2015
782.421649092—dc23
[B]

2015010849

ISBN 978-1-5011-0124-3
ISBN 978-1-5011-0125-0 (ebook)

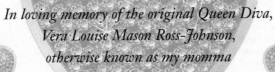

In loving memory of the original Queen Diva,
Vera Louise Mason Ross-Johnson,
otherwise known as my momma

Na, na, na, diva is a female version of a hustler.

—Beyoncé

I think most artists create out of despair. The very nature of creation is not a performing glory on the outside, it's a painful, difficult search within.

—Louise Berliawsky Nevelson

CHAPTER 1
THE GOSPEL

I FOUND CHURCH WHEN I was ten years old. It was the music that got ahold of me. At the time, 1988, my friends were checkin' for Michael Jackson, Atlantic Starr, and Bobby Brown. It was cool, but my momma was all about the gospel. "It's the Lord's music," she'd say. Momma never had to force church on me. Unlike so many kids in my neighborhood, I loved the sound of the choir, the drama of the sermons, the Sunday attire—all the fanfare that came with church. Mostly I loved the chance to be with my momma, Vera—and away from my stepdad, Donald.

My first time at Pressing Onward was right before Thanksgiving. Donald was getting on my last nerve. He got on my case for the smallest infractions—I drank too much milk, I didn't take out the garbage, I left the lights on. He'd badger my mom about how much she spoiled me. "Mind your own kids, Donald," she'd reply. But he persisted. Truth is, she never *really* told him off like I know my momma could.

One day Momma, Donald, and I were in the living room while I was grumbling about a homework assignment in which we had to write down all we were grateful for. I had managed a couple of things, but needed a few more and wondered aloud about it. Lawd, Donald jumped off the couch, looking like he wanted to deck me. "How you comin' in here and not know what to be grateful for?" he asked, his voice an octave too high for my liking.

"I didn't ask you," I responded, staring off at the blue-and-white plates hanging on the wall in the dining room.

He took a step toward me. "Who you talking back to?" Louder now; spit was flying.

I looked at Ms. V, but she said nothing.

I was tired of Donald picking on me, and of all the kids at school calling me a fat sissy. I decided it was time to run away. "I hate it here!" I shouted and slammed the door so hard a plate fell off the wall and shattered. I really had to run now. Those were Momma's favorite.

I believe God puts people in your life for a reason. I was fuming on the front steps, planning my getaway, when Denise Fountain walked by. Red and pink barrettes lined each side of her braided hair. "What are you doing, Freddie?" she asked as she approached me.

"Nothin'," I said.

"Why don't you come to church with me? Sunday is the Lord's day." Her voice was always a little squeaky.

I thought about it for a minute. "Which church?"

"Pressing Onward," she said. "It's fun."

"Sure," I said, standing up and skipping two steps to land on the sidewalk.

At church, I followed Denise down the long burgundy carpet of the center aisle until we got to the front pew. Denise pointed to a bald, heavyset man. "That's Pastor Squalls," she said. Then to a stylish woman with chocolate skin and a short, curly hairstyle. "And that's the choir director, Georgia."

The choir comprised eight women and an organist, or rather, a fabulous queen. His hairstyle was off the chain: he sported an immaculate fingerwave. I knew then that I wanted my hair that way one day. As they clapped and swayed in unison to songs like "Amazing Grace" and "True Praise," I felt my chest relax and all the chaos from the day start to dissipate. They absolutely hypnotized me with their timing, harmony, and—let's face it—their style.

What I didn't realize was how much I could actually *love* church—until I discovered Pressing Onward Baptist Church. It was right down the street from our house in Uptown New Orleans (in the Third Ward, not to be confused with the posh uptown) on Josephine Street. As a small child, I had passed it nearly every day, but the plain little brick building topped with a small wooden cross had never made much of an impression.

I decided I was going to sing in that choir. I eyed the lady with the roller set again and I decided that I would make myself useful enough to her that she'd have to let me sing. Before we left the church that day, I made a point to introduce myself to Georgia.

"Hello, Freddie," Georgia said. "I'm so glad you came to church today!" I liked her instantly. "And I sure hope you will come back next week."

"I will, Ms. Georgia," I said. And I meant it.

Denise walked me home that afternoon. When I walked through the front door, my momma was on the phone. The second she saw me she said, "Here he is, I'll call you back." She put the phone down and glared at me. "Come here, child," she said. I had to tiptoe over shards of blue-and-white porcelain to get to her. She grabbed my face in her hands. I thought she was going to smack me. "Boy, I'm so mad at you, I could whup your ass! I've been calling everyone looking for you." She pulled me in close and hugged me hard.

I realized she had been crying, and I felt terrible for making my momma worry like that.

"Sorry about the plate," I said, grabbing a broom from the closet and sweeping up the remains.

"Baby, don't ever leave this house without telling me where you are."

I wanted to tell her to tell her husband to get off my back, but I just said, "Yes, Momma."

"Where were you, anyway?"

"Church, Momma. Pressing Onward," I said. "I want to join the choir."

"Really? You never wanted to join the choir at my church."

"I know. There is something about this one," I said, hoping she wouldn't be offended.

"As long as you're going to church, baby, don't matter which one," she said.

Over the next six months, I attended the little brick church every Sunday. I discovered that there were lots of projects I could start, besides joining the choir. The first: helping to feed the neighborhood kids. There were so many skinny-ass kids with raggedy clothes walking around the uptown, I told Georgia, "We're a church. Let's feed the hungry. It'll get them to come to church too!"

Her eyes widened in surprise and she took a step back. "Fantastic, Freddie," she said.

I decided we'd host a "Feed the Kids" day every Saturday. It took a month to plan, but I loved keeping everyone on task. I drew up some flyers and plastered them all over the neighborhood. "Feed the Kids" fed these hungry children the stuff they craved—fried chicken, red beans, salad, and a slice of cake.

Next? I decided to raise money for a new stove. The one the church had was so old, it looked like it was from the thirties, and had only one working burner. I told Georgia I'd put on a Valentine's Fashion Show for the kids. "The boys and girls can model, and we will sell tickets for five dollars a pop."

"Freddie, no one has money to buy new clothes for a fashion show," she said.

"They don't have to buy anything new; they can wear what they have!" I answered, undeterred.

"I don't know, Freddie."

"Trust me, Georgia!" And she did. She let me plan a Valentine's Fashion Show fund-raiser that no one on Josephine Street will ever forget. Kids from the church wore their own clothes. Every last one of them was so excited to strut down the makeshift runway I had created by unrolling a giant roll of white paper in the backyard of the church. Proud parents beamed as I introduced each model. We raised around four hundred dollars from that show. Not only did we buy a new stove, but we had enough left over to paint the kitchen, too.

After the fashion show, Georgia kept me close, and I grew to love her like a mom. "You're special, Freddie," she would say, and my whole body would flutter with excitement. That support I was getting from the church gave my self-confidence a much-needed boost. I wasn't conscious of it at that age, but the unconditional welcome I was getting at Pressing Onward was something I wasn't getting anywhere else—not at home, not at school.

But my secret wish was that Georgia would hear my lovely voice and insist I join the choir. Finally, two months later, she brought up singing, but did so while throwing me a major-league curveball. "Freddie, we need some men in the choir for the tenor part. You wanna give it a try?"

"I'd love to," I said, tingling with excitement.

"But we'll need to do something about the fact that you're tone-deaf."

Huh? I thought. I felt like I had been karate chopped. "Tone-deaf?" I repeated, just making sure I'd heard her right. Maybe I wasn't Mariah Carey, but I did think I could hit a note.

"Yes, but it's not a big deal," she said. "That's a problem we can fix. We'll start you in the choir now, and we'll work together on your pitch after church."

The following Sunday, Georgia handed me one of those blue robes. I held it up to my nose, taking in the fresh detergent smell. I slipped it over my head and walked out behind the pulpit for the first time, alongside the other members. That new vantage point, looking out at the faces of the congregation, was positively electrifying. I knew most of the songs, so I was just concerned about my voice.

As we sang "Never Alone!" and "Oh How I Love Jesus," I forgot about Donald and those mean kids who hounded me about being an overweight sissy.

It wasn't just the lyrics; it was the way they were sung. I hope kids today understand the power of gospel music.

In time, Georgia became my godmom. We are close to this day. I spent so many weekends with her singing and cooking. She was gentle and kind.

And she was right about the practicing. Within a few months, my ear was near pitch-perfect. Also, I started to expand my range, learning to manipulate my vocal cords in ways I never knew possible, even from high falsetto to a low, booming bass. I started prancing around the house, singing loudly. It drove Donald nuts.

My momma noticed too. "Baby, you have a beautiful voice," she'd say. "Let's get you lessons."

"Yes, Momma, I'd love it." She found voice classes for me, and I started going once a week.

I started walking around Josephine Street belting out loud tenor sounds that would reverberate through the whole neighborhood. That's how I got to be known as the fat kid from Josephine with the funny operatic voice.

CHAPTER 2
POOPIE

Mᴜ ᴍᴏᴍᴍᴀ ᴜsᴇᴅ to joke that I came out of the womb "lookin' like a monkey."

I was born January 28, 1978, at Charity Hospital in New Orleans. I'm told I was covered with hair and had breasts when I arrived. Everyone laughed when my mom would tell (and retell) that story at family gatherings. But I always knew she loved me, and I absolutely adored her since my very first memory.

She was a thing of beauty, with a round face and naturally curved eyebrows framing her striking brown eyes. Her dresses hugged her long, lean physique like they were custom-made. As a very young boy, I'd watch her swirl rouge onto the apples of her cheekbones. If she caught me gawking, she'd dab the brush on my nose. "This is girl stuff, baby," she'd say. "Not for you!" But even then, it looked like an awful lot of fun.

Anyone who knows anything about me knows my momma was my heart. I don't know if it was because I was gay, so she took extra care with me, but we were tight from the get-go. My best friend, the transgendered Bounce artist Katey Red, once said I was like a baby kangaroo who never left her mom's pouch. Momma was the original Queen Diva.

Momma styled hair at Candy's Beauty & Barber Salon on Broad Street. She could handle old-school styles, weaves, updos, and fingerwaves, but nobody this side of the Mississippi did wraps and Jheri curls like my momma.

From nine in the morning to seven at night, she was at her station. She tried to instill beliefs in me: education, hard work, and never, ever letting people tell you who you are. Little did she know that later, when I became a teenager, that ethic would be put to the test.

Although she didn't share too much about her childhood, I know she was a force to be reckoned with. Born to Clarence Mason Sr. and Hazel Mason in 1960, she was one of six kids in Kenner, Louisiana, a suburb of New Orleans. Maybe when you have five brothers and sisters, you have to be loud or you won't be heard. My mom's brother, Uncle Clarence, who we call "Piece of Meat" (as a kid, he was always scrounging for scraps of meat), said that from the start she was the fiercest of them all. "Vera would say what's on her mind, whether you want to hear or not."

He said she got that fire from her mother, Hazel. One night, she stole her parents' car to go party in town. When she got home, Grandma Hazel was waiting for her with a switch.

Didn't stop my mom. She swiped that car the very next weekend, and after that, every chance she got. That also didn't stop Grandma Hazel from whuppin' her ass.

My momma was the center of our family. She was always doing everyone's hair and hosting throwdowns and cookouts. When it comes to delicious food in New Orleans, we don't mess around. Couldn't nobody touch her way with seasoning—crawfish, fried chicken, gumbo, étouffée. I lived for our family gatherings. "Go to your rooms," Momma would say to me and my sister and brother, and we'd obey. I'd hear howling laughter all night long coming from the kitchen. I'd find out later that she was getting high on herb with my aunts and uncles. That's how I grew up, surrounded by church, family, music, and food. And violence.

So many close friends and loved ones were murdered by gunfire. Like so many poor people in New Orleans, we struggled and fought on a daily basis and my family was no exception. Even though there was always a lot of love, sometimes Ms. V's love could be brutal. Her Southern Baptist beliefs did not include a tolerance for homosexuality. When those lips would purse, what came out of her mouth could be cruel, ya heard me? I'll just leave it at that.

I remember my childhood fondly, though. My father, Freddie Ross Sr., drove the most magnificent bobtail delivery truck for the grocery company Goodman & Beer. Between his and my mom's income, we did better than most around us. Most of my friends grew up in the projects, but Ms. V wouldn't settle for that.

Sometimes Daddy would let me sit in the driver's seat, even though the steering wheel was wider than my arms. When we'd roll down the street, I'd pull on the horn and the kids on the street would wave at us and just scream. I was the envy of every boy on the block.

At the store, I would beg him to take me in with him for a Drumstick ice cream cone with almonds. My dad teased me, because even then I would chat up all the giggling girls behind the counter. "You sure can talk for a four-year-old," he'd say.

I remember my dad as a soft-spoken, gentle man. He called me Poopie. It was just a nickname that stuck. People always said we looked a lot alike, but I can only see that when he smiles. We have the same mouth. He and Mom met through his sister in late 1975 and it was love at first sight. My momma was only fifteen at the time, but that didn't stop either of them. They married in 1976, then I came along two years later.

My parents separated when I was still too young to know why, but now I can see my momma was way too young to be married. She was still just a kid who wanted to go out on the weekends, and my dad wanted a wife at home. Even though I would have understood the word *divorce* at age four, I wouldn't have been able to accept it. At some point my dad just wasn't living with us anymore.

He'd still come by the house for me on weekends, though. Momma knew I missed him. "Your daddy's comin' for you," she'd say.

"Is it Friday yet?" I'd ask her every single day.

"No, baby, not yet," she'd reply.

Then he'd finally arrive at the door, "You ready, Poopie?" he'd ask, and I'd hop into his black 1969 Oldsmobile and we'd cruise together to my grandparents' house, Earth, Wind & Fire blasting from the car speakers. My paternal grandparents, Ruth and Frank Ross, lived in St. Rose, Louisiana, on the East Bank of the Mississippi River about thirty minutes west of New Orleans. Sometimes

I would be totally deflated when he'd leave me there for the weekend. I never knew where he went or what he did, but the message was loud and clear: do not ask. That rejection still stings, to this day.

Not that I didn't love my grandparents, especially my grandmother, Granny Ruth. She would cook the most savory mustard greens and corn bread and we'd eat it the old-fashioned way, with our hands. At night before I went to bed, she'd tuck me in, bringing me some milk and homemade sugar cookies. I thought I had died and gone to heaven.

I knew I was gay pretty much right from the start. I couldn't explain why, but I just felt different. If my fascination with singing, baby dolls, and my momma's hair care products weren't a dead giveaway, then the little flutter that surged through me when I saw cute boys—and not girls—was.

And from early on, I knew there was something very wrong with it. In my neighborhood, the message was loud and clear—faggots need not apply. The kids I knew who came out to their parents got kicked the hell out of their houses.

There were whispers about homosexuals around the projects, like Sissy Gina, Sissy Shannon, Ronnie, Too Sweet, Mark Tavia (who became my gay mom when I was a teenager), and Sissy LeRoy. We all knew and called them sissies amongst other gays and they were very respected in the neighborhood. But you couldn't walk around like today, talking smack about the guys who you want to suck off. Back then you'd be killed. I remember hearing people sneer about sissies and feeling that hole in my stomach because I knew that was me.

My brother Adam was born in 1982 to Adam Herman, a man my mother dated briefly. She was excited about it when she found out she was having another baby. And so was I. I couldn't wait to have a baby brother. I remember when she brought Adam home, I would stand over the crib all night trying to get a good look. The next year, my sister, Crystal, was born, by the same man.

One day, when I was five years old, I came home from school and my mom was folding laundry.

"Is Dad coming this weekend for me?" I asked.

"No, baby, he's not," she said, her head down. I couldn't tell what it was, but something was different.

"When is he coming?" I asked.

She dropped the shirt she had been folding and turned to me, her voice trembling. "Freddie, he's not. Your dad is gone, baby," she said. I felt it like a punch in my gut.

"Where did he go?"

"He got put away," she said.

"Where did he get put away?" I asked. I couldn't understand it. Like putting away clean clothes?

She got down on her knees and held my shoulders. "He got in trouble, sweetheart, and is going away for a while. Now, that's all you need to know." And when Momma spoke in that final way, I knew better than to beg her to tell me anything more.

But that didn't stop me from missing my dad every single day and looking for his truck to come rumbling down the street once more. I had no idea that I wouldn't see or speak to my father again until I was eighteen years old.

CHAPTER 3
DONALD DUCK

IN 1985, MY MOMMA met Donald Johnson. He was a stocky man with a peppered beard and mustache. Maybe Momma had a thing for truck drivers, because he was one too, for Coca-Cola. He was crazy about her. Right after getting together with Ms. V, Donald moved into our house. His two kids, Lil' Donald and Bianca, would come stay with us every summer.

I loved the idea of a big family, but from the start Donald favored Adam and Crystal and his own kids—and he didn't exactly like me. Of course, I eventually figured out that it was because I wasn't "boy enough," but at eight years old, I just wondered what I had done wrong. I was already dealing with the fact that I felt different, and having Donald on my case was a real annoyance.

One day Donald gave Crystal a brand-new Peaches 'n Cream Barbie doll. She came with a wonderful peach-colored sash and a fabulous matching bow in her hair. I was so green-eyed I could hardly breathe. Before Crystal even touched it, I had the doll out of its packaging. That night, we marveled at her shimmering peach gown.

When Donald peeked into the bedroom to tell us that dinner was ready, he spied me combing Peaches's long, blond hair. His eyes widened and his mouth set itself in an evil, straight line. "Freddie, why don't you go play ball outside with the rest of the boys?"

"I want to play with my sister," I replied, praying he'd leave me alone.

"Real boys don't play with dolls!" he bellowed, slamming the door hard.

Crystal looked shook. "Don't listen to him, Freddie," she said, carefully packing up the Barbie.

"Donald *Duck*," I muttered without even thinking. We both dissolved into a giggling fit so bad, I got a stitch in my side. From then on, that's what we called him behind his back.

"Donald Duck!" she said.

School was okay for me. I was naturally animated and talkative, so teachers liked me. Ms. McCoy at Mahalia Jackson Elementary School called on me to read the Pledge of Allegiance during an assembly. At five, I hadn't memorized the whole thing, but somehow I managed to get through it all by making up words and smiling. Everyone laughed, and I still remember the gratification that came with commanding an audience like that.

But that didn't mean kids didn't clown me. In first grade, these two boys, Willard and Tony, started in. "Freddie the fag!" Tony sneered, and then Willard knocked over my fruit punch. They kept up with that on the regular, and then other boys started to chime in with more of the same.

Thankfully, in second grade Momma moved me to Fisk-Howard Elementary, where within a week I had made myself indispensable to my teacher, Ms. Valmer. Cheerfully, I became her designated helper, organizing her worksheets, writing the day and date on the chalkboard, and passing out the morning snacks. At a parent-teacher conference, Ms. Valmer told my momma, "Freddie is going to do big things."

It almost balanced out being hazed for being feminine and fat.

One day my momma and Donald were sitting at the dining room table. I told them what Tony had said.

Momma shook her head. "You already know they just mean kids and not to pay them no mind."

But Donald had to chime in. "I told you, Freddie, what kind of boys walk around singing like a girl?"

"Mind your own kids," Momma snapped.

I was overweight my whole childhood too. I'm not sure exactly when I gained the weight, but I think all those ice creams with my dad didn't help. My momma was also a spectacular cook. Her Cajun gumbo and ghetto lasagna (all the ingredients of lasagna thrown together instead of layered) were delicious, but also comforting. I know I used to fix myself a few extra servings I didn't need. I can see now I was stuffing myself—and my feelings—but back then I figured it was baby weight.

As I approached my teens, I got fatter and the teasing intensified. Two things saved me: church and my uncle Percy. Percy Williams and my momma met through my uncle Ernest when I was ten. Blood is important, but where I come from, family are the people you ride or die for, ya heard me? A soft-spoken man with round-rimmed glasses, Percy was a gentle male figure in my life. And a consistent one.

I'm pretty sure Percy was born with flair. As a boy, he mastered a sewing machine and can stitch together anything, from gowns to drapes. He was a costume designer in the seventies for several New Orleans drag queens and is the go-to guy for customized Mardi Gras wreaths, coconuts, and parasols. I have a dressing room bursting with bedazzled jackets, airbrushed coats, and rhinestone-studded pants—all courtesy of my uncle. I know I inherited my fashion sense from my mom, but it was Uncle Percy who showed me how it's done.

We didn't talk about being gay until I got much older. Uncle Percy was from the generation where it was still very taboo. But I knew it like a baby animal knowing its own; it sure was comforting to have him around. I think that's part of why, unconsciously, I felt okay with my flamboyance from a young age.

After moving around to countless homes, in 1991 we finally settled in a green-and-white shotgun house on Josephine Street in Uptown New Orleans. It was the first home we'd stay put in for a good long while. It was modest, but most of my friends grew up in government housing projects. It was down the street from my aunt Debra's and it was on the nice part of Josephine Street, half a block down from where all the shootings happened.

And that's how I met Adolph Briggs. He lived in an apartment at the end of Josephine Street, with his mother, stepfather, and brother, in the same building as my aunt Debra. When I was thirteen he would become my best friend, and he is still one of the most important figures in my life.

It was fate one night that spring that brought us together, or maybe just Aunt Debra's unbelievably delicious stuffed bell peppers. Sometimes I could smell them from down the block, and my mouth would salivate thinking of how she baked them to perfection.

One night my mom was working late at the salon, and when I got home I was famished. I decided to take a stroll down Josephine Street and knock on my auntie's door. I could smell the beef and onions from the hallway and thought, I'm in luck. She opened the door wearing her apron.

"You got any supper?" I asked.

"I do, Freddie," she said, ushering me inside. When I got to the kitchen, there was a skinny little boy, maybe eight or nine, with a buzz cut, sitting at the table with a woman.

"I'm Freddie," I said, sensing I was gonna like this kid.

"Nice to meet you," said the cutest little queen I'd ever met, who added, "I'm Adolph." He offered his hand.

"Can I call you Addie?" I asked. Everyone got a nickname in New Orleans.

"Of course," he said smiling brightly. When his momma shot him a stern look, he looked down and fidgeted with his hands. It got quiet suddenly, until my aunt opened the oven and pulled out the candied yams and peppers. Addie started humming as we gathered around the table. My aunt placed the peppers on a big serving tray and set them on the table.

"Dig in," she said.

"Do you sing, Addie?" I asked, serving myself some yams.

"Oh no," he said, bashfully.

"I bet you do," I said. "You should come to church with me sometime and sing in the choir."

"Adolph can't," Addie's momma interjected before he could answer.

"Why, Momma?" Addie said.

"Because I say so," she said, shooting him a stare. Even at that age, I knew she was concerned about my influence on her son. But I didn't pay her any mind. I liked Addie, and knew us sissies was gonna be friends.

And we were. We had a lot more in common than being gays in the hood. We both had rotten stepdads. When Addie's father drank, his temper flared. I'd find out much later that Addie's stepdad and my stepdad, Donald, were friends, and that they purposely tried to keep me and Addie apart, scared that we would queer each other up.

A couple of weeks later, I called Addie's house. "Meet me around the corner of Danneel and Josephine," I said. "You're coming to church with me!"

"Yes, sir!" Addie said. We went to Pressing Onward that day. We sang "Silver and Gold" and "If You Come to Have Church." Swaying side to side with the choir, I watched Addie follow along from the pews. His eyes sparkled.

"I love your church, Freddie!" Addie said as we walked home that day. I liked that I was spreading the word of the Lord, but more than that, Addie came alive in that church.

"Girl, you can come anytime," I said.

Addie stopped dead in his tracks and put up his hand. "Freddie, don't call me girl. *Ever*," he said.

"You don't know you a fag?" I said. Addie stared back at me, mute. "It's okay," I added, putting my arm on his shoulder. "I'm one too." We continued down the sidewalk. Addie stayed silent, his head turned down.

I guess he wasn't ready to address it just then. "My momma and stepdad don't really want us playing together, Freddie," he said.

"Let's do this," I said. "When I belt out my deep operatic call, you answer in a high-pitched alto voice. That way, wherever we are—down the street, around the corner—we will know where were are." We practiced it a few times and that became our way to communicate if we couldn't get a hold of each other on the phone.

Addie stopped a couple of feet before his house. "Freddie, my stepdad would kill me if he thought I was gay," he said.

"I understand," I said, thinking, *Thank God for Momma, because I know if it weren't for her, Donald would probably kill me too.*

CHAPTER 4
JOSEPH

CARTER G. WOODSON MIDDLE SCHOOL. I was eleven years old. You should have seen this red-skinned boy shooting hoops. Those perfectly toned arms. The way those khakis hugged that round booty. Every girl in fifth grade had a crush on him, and so did I.

Outside of class, Joseph hung out mostly with the group of boys who played ball. So it was quite a surprise when we needed partners in science class and he picked me, especially since a lot of those same guys were calling me all kinds of names.

"Wanna come over after school and play Nintendo, Freddie?" Joseph asked one day in class.

"I'll ask my momma," I said, excited about the prospect of getting him all to myself for a few hours.

Ms. V agreed, so after school the following day, I went to his crib. It was a long apartment where you could see all the way down the hallway to a dusty piano.

"My mom won't be home for a while," he said, offering me a soda. "Let's go play," he said.

"Sure," I said, following him into a bedroom. I spied a small pile of video games on a table by the TV. I picked out Mario Brothers and Duck Hunter. When I looked over at Joseph, he was standing in front of his bed, staring at me. I felt a shiver from my head to my toes. Then he did something bold: he dropped his khakis to the floor. Through his tight-fitting white briefs I could see that his dick was hard. I didn't know what to do, so I remained perfectly still, clutching the record. It must have been about ten seconds, but it felt like an hour. Then he turned toward the window, pulled up his pants, and buttoned them up.

"My favorite is the Duck Hunters. Have you played it?" Joseph said, grabbing the game from me.

"No," I said. As the game came up on the screen, we talked about biology.

The next week, we had a project on electromagnetic energy. We were sitting on his bed, looking at the science book, when he rolled on top of me with his pants on. We rollicked around until we both had an orgasm.

His mother never seemed to suspect anything, nor did any of the girls at school who were dating him.

One of the last times I went to his house, we got close to having intercourse. We were in his bedroom, stripped down naked, when he turned me over. He was actually about to penetrate me when we heard the keys in the front door. We both jumped up and put our clothes on and returned to our study of cells.

"Damn it," he said, holding his crotch as if he were in pain. I strolled out to the living room and greeted his mom. With all my hormones raging and no one to talk to about it, I sprinted home that night as fast as my legs would take me.

"Momma!" I said, running into the kitchen as she was ironing Donald's shirts.

"Baby, what's wrong?" she asked, setting down the iron. "Are you okay?"

"I need some rubbers!" I blurted out.

My momma's lips pursed, and neither of us could believe those words had actually come out of my eleven-year-old mouth.

"What the fuck do you need rubbers for, Freddie?" she asked.

"I don't know," I said, looking down. "I just do?" It was too late to go back.

"I don't know what's gotten into you, baby," she said. "But you don't need no rubbers." She pressed the iron down so hard, I thought she was going to burn the shirt. "What's going on over at Joseph's? Do I need to call his momma?"

"No!" I shouted. "No, Momma, nothing is happening. I just heard if you kissed a girl, she could get pregnant."

She laughed and I thought, *Thank God, she believed me.* That Saturday I happened to be taking Momma her lunch at the salon when I spotted some rubbers in a big glass bowl. Just out there for the taking. I scanned the room. It was full of women chatting under the chair dryers and ladies in stylist chairs straightening their tightly coiled Afros. I made sure Momma wasn't watching and I grabbed a handful and stuffed them into my pocket. But Gloria, the receptionist, she'd had her eye on me from behind the desk. I stopped with my hand in the bowl.

"Take what you need, child," she said softly, turning to pull down a jar of Dixie Peach pomade for a customer. After that, whenever I'd go to the salon, Gloria would ask me if I needed more. I never actually used them with Joseph because after that night, Ms. V never let me go to his house again.

CHAPTER 5
COMING OUT

THE LAST SEMESTER of eighth grade, right before my thirteenth birthday my life changed for two reasons. One, the first Bounce song came out. And two? Well, we'll get to that.

Dances were the only part of school I took any pleasure in. It was January 1992 and I was getting ready for the first dance of the new year. That Saturday night, I took special care getting ready, especially because my new crush, Marc, was going to be there. My white polo shirt matched my new white Reebok Classics. I dabbed some activator gel on my newly buzzed flattop. And then I caught a glimpse of my stomach squeezed into my new blue jeans. My waist was a size 42. Damn it! I was a big, fat sissy. No way around it.

"You look beautiful, honey," Momma said as she came up behind me.

"Thanks, Mom," I replied.

Ms. V grabbed her keys and hollered out to me that we had to hit the road. We hopped into her old Ford Grand Marquis, which me and my sister and Adam called the Blue Lagoon, and she drove me to school. "You gonna ask Shatoney to dance?"

I tried to tell her, again, "No, Mom, it's not like that with us." Seemed liked nearly everybody except my mom and Shatoney herself knew I was gay.

I was resentful that I had to hide my gayness at home and felt guilty that the most important person in my life—my mom— would be the last to know. I couldn't live without her, that much I knew. I wondered if her fear of God was stronger than her love for me. I wanted to tell her so badly right then and there. My mind flashed to the older punks like Sissy Leroy and Shannon. I don't know how they dealt with all the hate back when they were growing up. Thank God for them because at least I had people who came before me to look up to.

I decided to just spit it out. My palms started to sweat.

"Well, who do you like, baby?" Momma asked.

I imagined Marc's deep chestnut eyes and his sturdy jawline, and my mouth was suddenly too dry to talk. I could see the school flagpole at the end of the street. This conversation would have to wait.

"No one, Mom, I don't want to date," I said.

She stopped the car and patted my arm. "I don't believe that, but you go on and have a good time," she said. "See you at eleven."

"Bye, Momma," I said. I stepped out of the car and slammed the door harder than I meant to.

I waved to Miss Harrison and Miss Smith as I entered the gym. Multicolored streamers were hanging from the gym ceiling. DJ Peewee had already set up his turntables below the basketball net and a few kids were already on the dance floor shaking to Run-DMC's "Peter Piper." I scanned the court for my best friend at school at the time, Antoinette, but she was nowhere in sight. So I walked over to the bleachers to wait for her.

Shatoney ambled in, all dressed up in a short pink skirt and some cute pink sandals to match. I wanted to run the other way but she looked right at me and broke into a shy, wide grin.

"Hi, Freddie!" she mouthed and blew me a kiss.

"Hi." I waved back. She walked with a dip over to me and leaned on the bleachers. Two boys in my class, Kevin and James, were watching her, their tongues practically on the floor.

She flounced down next to me in a suffocating cloud of White Diamonds perfume.

"You gonna dance with me tonight?" she asked. I felt terrible. She had long dancer's legs and perfect milk-white teeth, all of which was wasted on Big-Freedia-to-be.

"Yes," I said, trying to be a sport. Just then, Kevin and James walked over to the DJ. I knew they wouldn't acknowledge me, but I was desperate to escape Shatoney's obvious affections. I marched toward them, as if I had something important to tell them.

"Y'all heard that new song by MC T. Tucker and DJ Irv?" Kevin asked Peewee. The DJ held up a vinyl labeled "Where Dey At?" The way Kevin and James squealed piqued my curiosity.

By the early nineties, hip-hop was fast becoming mainstream across the country. Run-DMC, LL Cool J, and the Geto Boys were played on the radio and at house parties. But in proud New Orleans, we had our own sound—more stripped down, bass heavy, the topics more hard-core, like our lives. But this was way too explicit for school dances. Even Peewee knew it had to be cleaned up for a school dance.

The DJ was getting ready to drop the needle on the record and I was dying to hear it. And then, *boom!* It sounded through the speakers. Like nothing I had ever heard, it was that "Triggerman beat," which would become the blueprint of nearly every Bounce song. Shatoney was on it. She grabbed my hand and I couldn't help but follow her onto the floor with everybody else. Kids were waving their hands, shimmying and shaking like I had never seen my classmates do before. Marc was dancing with LaToya and I wanted to cut in, but I knew that wasn't gonna go over too well.

We must have danced for hours, one hip-hop song after another, until the dreaded slow jam came at the end of the night. Miss Smith turned down the lights. Peewee keyed up "Stay" by Jodeci and before I knew it, Shatoney had grabbed me around the waist and laid her head on my chest. Nothing to do, right, but relax and enjoy it. As we swayed back and forth, I watched Marc and LaToya.

> *Tonight, let's start our love again*
> *Tonight, we can be more than just friends,*
> *Don't you know, the sun it is going down,*
> *Stay for a little while.*

The next thing I knew I was hard as a rock. Where did that come from? I tried to pull away, tried to force myself to think of something else, but it was too late. I was aroused and there was nothing I could do. Don't think Shatoney didn't notice. This was sending the wrong message to her, but my whole body had responded in a way that totally surprised me.

When the song ended, I started to pry myself loose. "Gotta run, baby," I said to Shatoney. She looked like she was about to cry, so I stepped back and hugged her. "See you Monday," I said, feeling like a cad.

I walked downstairs and saw Ms. V was out back smoking a cigarette, so I called Addie about that song "Where Dey At?"

"You hear that song by MC T. Tucker?" I asked.

"Yes, bitch! 'Where Dey At?'" he said. "Where you been?"

"Come over in thirty," I said. "When my mom leaves, we can go to Peaches," I added, referring to a local record store. This was the start of me buying all the local rap I could get my hands on.

At Peaches, I bought a copy of the record on cassette with the money I had saved from my allowance. Addie also urged me to get "Putcha Ballys On" and he bought "Pop That Thang." Both were new tracks by Bust Down, an artist from the Ninth Ward. When we got back to the house, we put "Where Dey At?" on my mom's phonograph. I couldn't believe the explicit lyrics. *Fuck David Duke, fuck David Duke, I said, I said, I said. I said, Fuck David Duke, fuck David Duke.* It was raw. It was explicit—*Dog-ass ho better have my money.*

We were transfixed because it was so defiant, so wrong. And apparently we weren't the only ones who thought so. "Where Dey

At?" turned out to be a huge moment in Bounce history. It was the song playing at every house party that year, pumping out of every car and boom box.

But what made it different from everything else—and significant—was that it sampled that Showboys beat. The Triggerman beat made its way into numerous New Orleans rap songs after that and that's what makes it a Bounce song. I don't know why we love that beat so much. Maybe because it's reminiscent of big-band jazz sound and parade traditions. Either way, it would become the defining sound of Bounce music. If it has the Triggerman beat, it's Bounce!

"Where Dey At?" was such a local sensation that a year later in New Orleans my boy DJ Jimi covered the song. His version was more polished, and in 1992 it landed on the *Billboard* rap charts, which was huge: New Orleans was starting to make an impact on a genre completely dominated by New York and Los Angeles.

We played "Where Dey At?" for hours that night. When it was time for my mom to come home, I slipped the cassette under my mattress. My momma didn't have a problem with mainstream hip-hop but the F-bomb and the N-word were off-limits (even if she did say those words herself from time to time). My momma could be a mess of contradictions, and you just had to roll with it and figure out which rule she was running with at the time.

A FEW WEEKS LATER, my mother had big plans for my thirteenth birthday party. Outside, in the backyard, she had decorated some foldout tables gold and black with carnation centerpieces. Tied to the backs of chairs and on our trees were black and gold ribbons and lots of matching balloons. When I came out of my room to help, Whitney Houston's "I'm Your Baby Tonight" was blasting out of the speakers. The whole family—Crystal, Adam, Aunt Betty, Aunt Debra, Uncle Percy, Aunt Dawn, Donald, his kids, my cousins Leonard and Junior, Addie and his momma—were invited.

As people arrived, the pile of gifts on my table grew. I was lighting candles when Addie walked outside.

"Come on," I said, and waved him over. We walked into the kitchen, where I hoped to steal a moment with him. "I'm gonna tell her today."

Addie's eyes got big. "Oh, Freddie, your momma gonna kill you." I could see the fear in his eyes.

"I don't think so," I said, more to myself.

"You sure you ready?" he asked.

"It's time," I said. "I can't hide anymore." Just then, Aunt Debra walked into the kitchen.

"Happy birthday, sweetie!" she said, putting her famous gumbo into the refrigerator and moving on to join the rest of the guests in the back.

Addie looked at me and said, "You're so brave, Freddie."

We went outside and I took my place at one of the tables. Momma had cooked for three days straight. The tables were loaded with all my favorites—grilled crawfish, fried chicken, smoked sausage, and deviled eggs.

After dinner, Crystal and Ms. V came out of the house together holding up the most magnificent vanilla cake from McKenzie's bakery. It was square and covered in blue, green, and white frosting. Everybody sang "Happy Birthday." As they placed it in front of me, I took a huge breath and blew out the candles—my wish was that one day, I could be myself.

Afterward we all danced and sang again, this time to my mom's favorite Frankie Beverly & Maze album. At one point, I looked over at Ms. V and she was sitting alone. It was my moment. I was practically too big to do so, but I climbed on her lap like I had been doing all my life.

"You having fun, baby?" she asked.

"Mom, I'm gay." Just like that, I said it.

She just looked into my eyes for the longest time without either of us saying anything, but my heart was pounding so hard I thought I'd faint. I couldn't tell if she was irate or not since half the time when she was mad her face didn't move. "Baby, I already know," she finally whispered.

"You do?" I said, jumping off her lap.

"Yes, child," she responded. I stood completely still waiting for her to rage at me or yell that I was going to burn in hell, but she didn't. She just stood up, hugged me hard, and said, "God got you." Then she walked over to the table and sliced herself a piece of cake.

It was as if nothing had happened. It seemed to me there was some unusual whispering between my aunt Debra, my sister, and my mom, but no one, except Crystal, said a word to me.

"Freddie, everything is gonna be okay." She came up to me as I was finishing off some soda. I didn't know what to think, but my sister's reassurance was critical that night. I always knew Crystal was down for me.

Now, my momma. Could she be waiting to punish me later? I knew it wouldn't just be forgotten.

I crawled into bed that night, full on corn bread and cake, feeling strangely serene that it had finally been said.

As Momma passed my room, she poked her head in the door. "Happy birthday, Freddie," she said.

"Good night, Momma." I replied. After she had gone, I pulled my blanket over my head and prayed. *Dear God, I know this is hard for Momma. Please help her understand.*

The next morning, Ms. V came in and sat on the edge of my bed. Her eyes were red and swollen. "Is it something I did?"

"Momma! No, of course not," I reassured her.

"Did someone hurt you?" she asked.

"Momma. Nothing happened. God made me like this."

Tears streamed down her pretty brown cheeks. "You're choosing a difficult path, baby. But it's your life," she said.

I took both her hands in mine. "That's just it, Momma," I said. "I didn't choose this. I have been this way since I was born."

She shook her head like she didn't believe me. "That's not what God says, but I love you no matter what anybody says," Momma responded. I felt relief and fear at the same time. Relief that she wasn't going to throw me out, but also apprehension because I knew what she was saying about a difficult path was right.

A couple of weeks after my birthday party, Sissy Shannon was found dead by police in Van Mac Park. She had been beaten and a broomstick had been shoved up her ass. In no time, the news made

its way throughout the projects. Came to find out, she was murdered by a guy who thought he was going to be exposed as her
lover. I don't know if my mom knew about it or not. We never
spoke of it. Poor Shannon. She paved the way for sissies like me,
and for that she's a hero in my book.

CHAPTER 6

WALTER L. COHEN HIGH SCHOOL

IN SEPTEMBER 1992, I started at Walter L. Cohen High School. I was just grateful to be going to high school, since more than half the kids from Josephine Street—including Addie—didn't get that far. Of course, I was apprehensive about the fact that I was an overweight sissy, but I prayed that high school would be different from middle school. At fourteen, I was out, and I didn't want to hide anymore. Cohen was going to be a fresh start: older kids, new teachers, and a much wider world.

The day before school, I had gone with Momma to Maison Blanche department store, where I bought a black briefcase. I meant business. "And I gotta have these, Momma!" I said, holding up shiny brown dress shoes to go with the school uniform of khaki pants and a white button-down shirt. Ms. V's eyes widened when she saw the price tags on those two items, but she opened her wallet without a word.

Cohen High sprawled the entire length of a city block. A few windows needed repair and the hallways needed a fresh coat of paint, but I was bewitched from the second I set foot on campus. I marched into English that day, sporting my flattop and totin' that briefcase like it contained secret CIA documents. I settled in the very front row, where I had to crane my neck up to take in the very imposing six-foot-two Miss Stokes. She did not play. Soon I would learn that all the kids respected her, even the tough ones. She could be warm, though, too and I decided to be her pet. So, in typical Freddie fashion, I created a job for myself. I organized her worksheets, quizzes, and tests into manila folders that I labeled with a Sharpie, and arranged her pencils and pens according to color.

Once she walked into the classroom to find me at the pencil sharpener, working on a stack of No. 2 pencils. "Thank you, Freddie," she said, giving me one of her rare smiles. "You're going to go far in life because you know how to make yourself useful."

I was only getting fatter, too. My waist had ballooned to fifty-two inches! And what always motivates a fat kid? Food, of course. So when I discovered Miss Stokes ran a snack shop in the closet in the back of her classroom, stocked with potato chips, pickles, brownies, World's Finest chocolate bars, and sodas, it was over. She was raising money for senior trips and such, and I was soon put in charge of tracking and selling snacks, collecting the money, and guarding the closet.

As soon as kids got wind of it, they were always trying to pilfer chocolate and sodas. But I wasn't kidding when it came to my job, hear me? One time, Vincent, this big football player, crept over and tried to swipe a chocolate bar when Miss Stokes had her back turned. I grabbed a ruler and whapped his hand hard. "Put that back," I hissed, holding up the ruler, threatening to swat him again. This was all happening inches away from the desk of one of the most beautiful girls in my class, Yolanda Gaines, who was watching the entire exchange.

"Faggot," Vincent said before tossing the bar back at my head. I ducked just in time.

"Who you callin' faggot, Vin?" Yolanda stood up from her chair, placing a hand on her shapely hip. Vincent dropped his eyes and didn't say a word.

By that point, Miss Stokes had noticed the to-do. "What's going on over there?" she asked.

"Nothing, Miss Stokes," Vincent answered, slinking back to his desk. She looked at me for confirmation.

"Everything is just fine," I said, saving his ass. He'd have his day.

"Don't make me send you all to Mr. Grey," she said. "The principal isn't gonna like it." I was more angry at Vincent for getting me in trouble with Miss Stokes than about the comment. The next day, Miss Stokes brought a silver padlock to class. "Freddie, keep this somewhere safe," she said, placing the key in my palm.

"Of course, Miss Stokes," I said, flipping open my briefcase and tucking it inside the first pocket.

Despite the occasional homophobic athlete or thug, I learned that my "difference" actually made me more popular at Cohen, especially with girls. My first friends were Kendra, this lanky girl with piercing green eyes, and Idella, a petite thing with the most marvelous jumbo braids. They were cheerleaders. At Cohen High, the Hornets were a central part of school culture; the cheerleaders were a central part of the Hornets.

Kendra was always breaking out in cheers. "Gimme a *C*! Gimme an *O*! Gimme an *H*!" she'd yell, eventually spelling out *Cohen*. I absolutely loved to watch the girls practice. There was something magical about those cheers and those green-and-black uniforms! I started wondering what it might be like to be a cheerleader myself. I had the voice for it, but I had also packed on a lot of extra pounds.

What if a boy joined the squad? It wasn't totally unheard-of. The No Limit Records rapper Mystikal, who attended Cohen before me, was said to have been a fierce cheerleader. There was also this sissy from the Magnolia projects who Addie hung with, named Vockah Redu. Vockah danced for the Booker T. Washington High dance troupe, the Pep Squad. Being the first boy to make the team, he got a ton of attention—from the radio and local newspapers.

While Kendra and Idella tried out and made the team, I helped them with their cheers and moves during recess and lunch. Practicing their moves in front of my mirror at home, I longed to join in, but I didn't have the nerve just yet.

Academically, I did okay in school my first year. It didn't come easy, but I managed to get B's and C's. I loved my history teacher, Miss Strickland, and my algebra teacher, Miss Cesar. It wasn't the subjects I loved so much as it was the teachers, and I always wanted to please them.

FRESHMAN YEAR I came out to my mom. Sophomore year I came out to the world, ya heard me? From the start, I was rocking freezes and finger waves. I got most of my ideas for hair from the hair shows Ms. V would take me to. I saw men sporting wraps and bobs and all I could think was, Baby, how am I gonna come with mine?

Even though my momma was doing those very dos on her clients' hair, I wasn't about to ask her to do mine. I didn't want to push it. Joe from the choir did everyone's hair, so one day after church, I asked if he might do mine.

"Sure, Freddie," he said. "We'll get your hair laid, honey." A couple of days later, Addie and I caught the bus to Joe's shop. "Come sit in the chair," Joe said, checking out my flattop. "How about a nice little freeze?" he asked, turning on the curling iron.

"Sounds wonderful," I said, wondering how he was going to transform this stout sissy. He went to work for about an hour, combing out my curls. I made it a point not to look in the mirror until it was done. When it came time to check it out, I was floored! My hair was sticking up, practically touching the ceiling, and I had a big gold streak up the middle.

"Girl, it's beautiful!" Addie said. I went home that night feeling like a swan, until I remembered I had to get past Momma.

When I walked through the living room that night, she was watching TV. But I could see out of the corner of my eye that she had spied my do. I set my briefcase down by the couch. "Okay, Freddie," she finally said, calmly. "Where you get that done?"

"Joe from church," I said.

"It's too high," Ms. V said. She clicked off the television. *Oh no*, I thought, *is she gonna start with me?* "But, baby, you do you."

"Thanks, Momma!" I said, overjoyed that she seemed to be okay with it. I sat in my room that night staring into the mirror and thinking: *How is this hair gonna fit into Ms. V's new Chevy Astro van?*

I couldn't wait for school the next day. I was ready fifteen minutes early and waited by Ms. V's van for my ride. She came out and unlocked the doors. I had to tilt my head over to one side to get into the van and I rode sideways all the way to school.

"See, that shit is too high!" she said, laughing.

"Love you, Momma," I said, hopping out of the car.

"Love you too, baby," she said. I walked into school rocking my freeze with the gold streaks! I was so proud. I strutted down the hallway of school like it was a runway. And heads did turn. George, this straight kid who had never even noticed me before, hollered, "Whoo-whoo!"

Someone whistled.

Then someone else yelled, "Marge Simpson!"

"Freddie!" Kendra was suddenly in front of me. "You look amazing! Who did that?"

"Joe," I said as we walked toward homeroom.

"Freddie, your hair is jacked to the ceiling!" this girl Marilyn said. After that, I went from well liked to mad popular. Everybody wanted to be around the kid with the wild hair. That was a life-changing moment. I mean, here I was, once the fat sissy in middle school, but now in high school suddenly everyone was admiring me. I felt completely high from all the sudden interest, all that positive attention, I realized, I could create for myself.

In December, Kendra and Idella were chatting in the cafeteria about the upcoming cheerleading tryouts for the new year when I sat down with my tray. "Freddie, why don't you try out for the squad?" Kendra asked.

"A sissy on the Hornets Squad?" I asked, feeling tingles all through my body.

"Why not?" asked Idella. "We need someone to hold up the girls." She said tryouts started the next week and would run all week long.

"Okay," I finally said. I sure was big enough.

"Great!" said Kendra, "Let's practice the routines after school today." I agreed and proceeded to rehearse routines in my head during math and history.

After school, I met up with Kendra and Idella outside the gym and we practiced for hours: "We are superior, we are standing on top! We are number one, we can't be stopped!" They also taught me the jumps, kicks, and cartwheels. Like church had done, cheering—with its moves and rhythm—would serve as a training ground for what would become my shows.

When it came time for tryouts, there were forty girls and two boys (in addition to me) who were trying out for twelve spots on the team. We would all do the cheers and numbers together and then the coach, Ms. Thomas, would come around and watch. It was so nerve-racking, especially when I was with kids who weren't coordinated or couldn't remember cheers. There was this girl Wanda who had the hugest and most unwieldy melons. She wasn't very graceful, honey. One time, she tried to do a cartwheel and landed straight on her head.

"Girl down!" I said loud enough for Kendra to hear. We doubled over in laughter. I think that was the first time I said it, but it wouldn't be the last. After that, it became one of my catchphrases.

A week after rigorous tryouts, Coach Thomas said she was going to read off the list of kids who made the starting team, and that everyone who didn't make it could come to practice. She read the names Kendra and Idella. Then Damien and Trent. Then the last name: Freddie Ross. I was over the moon! I don't even remember how I got home.

"Momma! Momma!" I ran inside the house calling out. "I made the cheerleading squad!"

"I knew you were gonna make it, baby!" she said. "You always will!"

CHAPTER 7
IN DA CLUB

ADDIE WAS ALWAYS up on the new shit. He would go on constantly about new stuff, like when Take Fo' Records, the first Bounce label, signed DJ Jubilee. "And wait till you see his dancers!" he said.

That week, Addie had discovered a rapper named Ms. Tee, who he claimed was fresh as hell. Ms. Tee was signed to a local label called Cash Money, started by two brothers, Ronald and Bryan Williams, from the Magnolia projects. There was a ton of buzz about Cash Money, but who knew they were about to become one of the fiercest labels in hip-hop? Addie heard her on New Orleans's FM station Q93's *9 Songs at 9*, a weekly national radio show where DJ Wild Wayne would play nine songs from local artists. Addie came over to the house one morning, rapping Ms. Tee's lyrics and mimicking her gestures.

A week or so later, on a balmy July night, Addie called and said he was going to come over and pick me up. "It's going down, let's go!" he said.

"Where?" I asked.

"Girl, we're going to the club!" My heart skipped a beat. I was dying to see what the clubs were all about. The fact that Ms. V was out with Donald that night meant there was a chance that I could sneak out and be back before they got home. If I was wrong and I got caught, there would be hell to pay. My momma didn't mind me attending the block parties and school dances, but at fifteen years old, the clubs were strictly forbidden. That said, it wasn't like Ms. V hadn't done the same thing when she was my age. She admitted to me that she used to steal her parents' green Chevy Impala at night by shifting the gear into neutral and silently rolling backward out of the driveway. Then she'd go into town to party.

Since I had still said nothing, Addie added: "Yo, Freddie. You coming with me?"

"Come by in thirty," I said and hung up the phone. I scanned my closet for something nightclub appropriate. Humming to Mary J. Blige's "Real Love," I settled on a white T-shirt with blue jeans. As I slipped on my new Timbs, I thought the best I could hope for at that point was to blend in.

I heard Addie's footsteps outside a little after ten o'clock. As soon as I opened the door, he blew past me, in dark blue jeans and with a small duffle bag slung over his shoulder.

"I need to use y'all's bathroom," he said, looking around intently. Before I could answer, he slipped into the bathroom and shut the door. A couple of minutes later he walked out in baby blue shorts that barely covered his skinny little ass and a pink shirt.

"Bitch, where are you going like that?" I asked.

"To see Ms. Tee!" he said.

"Your ass looks big, baby," I said, noticing that his booty looked fuller.

Addie pulled the elastic band of his shorts. "I got two pairs of briefs under here, baby," he declared proudly.

"Girl, who are you trying to convince you aren't gay?" I said.

"Let's go," he said, ignoring my comment. We talked the entire five blocks to the club. Right before we got there, Addie turned serious. "When you see the bouncer," he instructed, snapping his fingers, "just act like you belong, baby."

"What if they ask about my age?" I asked. My hair was on point, but we were both underage, after all.

"They won't," he said confidently. As we approached the club, the thundering bass was blasting all the way down St. Andrew Street. A handful of girls stuffed into skintight skirts were lingering outside the door. *Shit*, I thought, *they look way older than me.* I felt ultra uncool in my blue jeans. Even Addie was dressed to impress.

My chest tightened as I followed Addie. He marched past the bearish bouncer, who waved us inside. Turned out, Addie was right. I had no problem getting in that night or any other night in what became regular trips over the next few years. Looking back, I think it's because I was so fat that no one could tell my age. Addie, on the other hand, got in that night, but baby, he got kicked out so many times during our clubbing stints, it's not even funny. It would drive him crazy, but that night these two sissies traipsed right in without so much as a word.

Club 2001 was a dark and smoky place with low ceilings. Tag Team's "Whoomp! (There It Is)" was blasting out of the speakers so aggressively, that I thought my eardrums might burst. Addie started saying something I couldn't hear. As he spoke, I took it all in: Everyone in my periphery was bouncing along to the beat, so I did too. Boys were blinged out in gold chains. Most of the girls had a lot of skin showing, four-inch heels, and makeup till Tuesday. Thank God I had my freeze and my boots, or I would have been laughed out of the place in five minutes.

"Let's get a drink," Addie said, then ushered me to the bar. "Two pineapple and vodkas," he said to the bartender. Sounded good to me. Truth was, I had had liquor at my house before with my mom. It wasn't anything I ever cared much for and I certainly never overindulged in it. Let's just say it wasn't my drug of choice. A drink on occasion was, and still is, standard.

I leaned against the bar as the DJ dropped DJ Jubilee's "Do the Jubilee All . . ." I think the chorus, *Shake baby shake shake shake shake / Twerk baby twerk*, made it the first recorded song to use the term *twerk*. Girls suddenly started screaming and shaking their asses at lightning speed. By that point booty shaking was a regular move at the school dances, so it was no surprise to see it at the clubs. Simply put, twerking is an ass-shaking dance from the New Orleans projects.

Addie started to cut up! He had moves, like the bend-over and the booty-shake, or the twerk. But the move that got him attention was the swiggle-wiggle, where he would gyrate his pelvis and booty while moving his feet so quickly he would go in circles around the room. The crowd went nuts, stepping back and making a space for him. When Addie jumped onto the floor facedown—still twerking—girls formed a circle around him and started clapping.

In plain sight, couples were making out; in fact, in the dark recesses of Club 2001, there were people doin' a lot more than that. The atmosphere of raw sex utterly shocked me, but I liked it.

Ms. Tee didn't hit the stage until about midnight, but it was worth the wait because she turned it up. I was standing in the back of the club when she jumped onstage rocking dookie braids pulled up in a bun on the top of her head and gigantic hoop earrings. She couldn't have been more than fifteen years old, but she exuded confidence as she performed "I Don't Give a Fuck" and "Fuck Niggaz and Fuck Hos." Her lyrics were more intricate than any of the Bounce music I'd heard up to that point—they were actually stories—and her attitude was raw as fuck.

We filed out of the place at nearly 2 a.m. Addie rapped Ms. Tee's "I Don't Give a Fuck" all five blocks home. Suddenly, Ms. V ran through my mind and I felt my nerves tingle. Thankfully, her car was nowhere in sight when I got to the house, so I waved to Addie and snuck back in without a problem. I crawled into bed that night, ears ringing and my clothes drenched in the smell of smoke. I was changed forever. I wanted to go again. I wanted to be up there, like Ms. Tee.

BY MY THIRD YEAR OF HIGH SCHOOL, I was rocking curls and claws (a style where you curl your hair and claw it out with a comb). It was also the year I discovered my momma's closet full of handbags and decided to trade in my briefcase for a purse. I snuck into her room one day after school and pulled out all the elegant totes—the olive-green suede, light pink faux leather, white patent leather hobo, vintage lace—and lined them up on her bed. She had every shape and color. I spied a black shoulder bag with a pocket on the outside. It was almost a box shape, and so out of all of them, it looked the most masculine. I held it out in front of me and then put it over my shoulder. I put all the bags back except that one. As soon as Ms. V walked through the door from work, I showed it to her.

"Can I have this?" I asked, holding it up.

"What's wrong with your briefcase?" she asked.

"Nothing, I'll still use that," I said. "But I need another bag for my uniforms and yearbook stuff."

"What about a backpack, baby?"

"I like this one," I said, smiling sweetly so she couldn't resist.

Momma looked right into my eyes as if to say "Why, baby?" But instead she said, "Fine."

Once I carried it to school that first time, it became a permanent fixture on my arm.

Just as I was coming into my own with my cheerleading and freezes, I ran into a little snag.

One night near the end of sophomore year, I was eating dinner with Ms. V when the telephone rang. Momma picked up the call. "Good evening, Mr. Grey," I heard her say. Oh no, I thought. Mr. Grey was my principal. This couldn't be good. I had been so consumed with cheering, I hadn't quite focused on my classes, but I didn't think I was failing.

"He is?" she said, pursing her lips like she did when she was about to go off. "Freddie's hair is distracting to the kids?" I sank down in my chair. That was it; Ms. V was gonna put an end to my fancy dos, I was sure. And then, "Well, Mr. Grey, you need to tell your students not to worry about Freddie's hair. My boy is at school to learn," she added, "and they need to be doing the same!" And she slammed the phone down on my principal.

When Ms. V came back to the table she asked, "You want another piece, Freddie?"

"No thank you, Momma," I said.

She kissed my forehead. "Go out there and tell them who you are, Freddie," she said. That was huge for me. Not only did my mom accept that I was gay, but she had my back.

BY JUNIOR YEAR, I really started to excel. My grades had gone from B's and C's to A's and B's. I worked hard, and once I got the hang of studying, school got easy for me.

I had also become totally immersed in cheering, for all the predictable reasons: the physicality, the camaraderie, and the competition. By junior year, I was captain of the boys' team and cocaptain of the girls'. But more than all that, cheering got me the kind of attention I craved.

At that time, I also wanted extra cash for certain things, like my hair and clothes. There was no way Ms. V was going to fund my new preoccupation with fashion and makeup, so that year I got my first real job, at the Burger King down the street from our house. When I went to fill out the application, I eyed the cute blue uniforms. When they called me a few days later to ask if I could start that week, I was elated! From Burger King to Bounce Queen, who knew?

"I'm so proud of you," Ms. V beamed when I told her. "That's my child!" They started me out as a sandwich maker. All the managers were women and, just like with my teachers, I went the extra mile to please them. I organized the cleaning supply closet. Some kids would come to work in the dark blue pants with the wrong shirt or the light blue shirt with the wrong pants, but not me. I wore the matching uniform set every shift with pride. Within six months, the manager, Ms. Gloria, called me into the back office after work.

"Freddie, we think you have what it takes to work at the register," she said. "We'd like to start training you next week."

"Yes, ma'am!" I said, excited to tell my mom of the promotion. Standing behind the cash register meant chatting up customers, my specialty! You better believe I made sure that every child who came in got the Burger King crown with his or her Kids Meal. In no time, all the parents and kids would practically fight to line up at my register. And I rocked that Burger King crown with pride, baby.

But while I was thriving in school and work, home life with Donald Duck was deteriorating. He was always on my case about something and it was obvious that he didn't ride his own kids like he did me.

One night it came to blows. I had walked into the living room while he and Ms. V sat on the couch watching TV. "Close that light off, Freddie," he told me. Before I could even get my hand on the switch, he leapt up from the couch and just started wailin' out, yelling and screaming: "I told you to turn off the light, you heard me?

How fucking long does it take for you to turn the damn light off?" He was going on and on, and suddenly all the pain and anger I had from all those years of his shit just came to a head. I pulled my fist back and clocked him as hard as I could in the face. It was the first time in my life I punched anyone. Donald wasn't about to let a sissy beat him up, so he started punching back, and the next thing you know, we were rolling around on the living room floor in a brawl. Ms. V was hollering for Donald to stop. She finally jumped in the middle of us and so I had to stop. I stood up. I was breathing hard and my lip was bleeding. And then Ms. V pursed her lips and walked over to Donald. "You put your hands on my kid again," she said, pointing her finger into his face, "I'll fuck you up." She looked at me. "Freddie, go pack your clothes," she said.

I've never seen Momma so mad at Donald, I thought, as I filled up a bag of T-shirts and blue jeans. Ms. V came by a few minutes later with Adam and Crystal by her side and took us to my aunt Debra's house. Crystal cried all the way there. She had grown to love Donald, and to this day she considers him her father.

Donald would call my momma every couple of days and beg her to come back. "Don't you touch my kids," I heard her say a few times. Crystal would ask every few days if we were going to go back. I felt guilty for putting Ms. V and Crystal through all this, but Lawd, I was so relieved to be away from him for the next month.

To make things worse for my momma, while we were at Aunt Debra's Mr. Grey called her at least four more times about my hair. "Them kids need to worry about their books," she defended me. Then, one day, Mr. Grey called her at work and demanded that she come to his office and talk to him. She was furious at him, but she got into her van and came to school. After doing that twice more, she couldn't take it any longer.

"Baby, I'm losing money every time the school calls me and I have to go down there and explain your hair to them."

"I understand, Momma," I said, deflated that she had to give in.

"We're gonna take that out tonight, before I leave, ya heard me?" Ms. V said, wiping her hands on her apron.

"Yes, Momma," I said. Later that night, she stuck my head under the sink and washed out the most gorgeous finger waves I had ever had.

Two months later, Ms. V told me, Crystal, and Adam to pack up our things and wait in Aunt Debra's living room. Donald came by, and we piled into the car and rode back home in silence. My family wasn't much for talking things out. Not a word was said about the fight and we went back to business as usual.

CHAPTER 8
TOTALLY SISSIFIED

BY MY SENIOR YEAR of high school, I was totally sissified. Caesar hairstyles (the brushed-forward short haircuts that were the same length all the way around) were all the rage, and with my new clutch and cherry lip gloss added to my daily repertoire, I was a Queen Diva in the making.

It was time to think about college. Most of my friends weren't even going to apply, but I knew Ms. V wouldn't stand for that. I had one friend, Peter, who was going to college, and he told me about the University of Louisiana at Lafayette. "They have a good nursing program," Peter said to me as we were perusing the catalog in the high school library one day. Taking care of people came naturally to me, so just like that, I applied to nursing school.

By high school, Georgia from Pressing Onward and I had grown very close. She was like a second mother to me and I started to call her "Grandma." I was honored beyond belief when she made me assistant choir director. That meant I supervised rehearsals, taught everyone their parts, and made sure members knew what to wear and what time to be where.

I also started conducting the choir, which meant I learned all the claps, gestures, and signals. This was the beginning of what I would later come to do onstage. Only now I conduct my shake team of dancers and my audience. I got so immersed in the choir at this point that other groups around the city were getting wind of me.

I also started to travel to gospel music conferences in cities like Minneapolis, Indianapolis, and Atlanta with other church members; we'd learn new hymns and return with new sheet music. Besides the hair shows I went to with my momma as a kid, these were my first trips outside New Orleans. A lot of kids I knew had never been outside their ward, so for me to travel like this opened up a whole world; it helped make me adaptable and open to new experiences.

Another part of church that I came to love was fellowship with other churches. I mostly remember the different dance groups, like a Jesus drill team, which would march in these fabulous military-style outfits and, in perfect formation, yell, "One, two, three, four, Jesus!" These men blew me away.

This was when I started to think that I might have a future in gospel singing, for real. "Freddie, God gave you a gift with that voice," Ms. V would say. "Use it wisely."

While I was becoming more absorbed with church, Addie's escape was Bounce. By then our New Orleans version of rap was in full swing. Every ward and project was being represented in the clubs and at block parties. It was 10th Ward Buck and Jubilee from the St. Thomas projects, Partners-N-Crime from the Seventeenth Ward on Big Boy Records, and UNLV (which stood for "Uptown Niggas Living Violently"), who released *6th and Baronne*, a huge hit in 1993 on Cash Money Records. Juvenile was a young kid making music who would later become one of Cash Money's biggest-selling artists of all time.

All types of female rappers were starting to bubble, too. In addition to Ms. Tee, there was Mia X and Magnolia Shorty. Then there was this saucy emcee Cheeky Blakk, who released the song "Twerk Something!," which started a fierce rivalry between the two artists. Bounce was becoming very real.

Local artists were big, and where I come from we support our own, so there was a huge demand for them. Clubs like Sam's, the Focus, and Escape quickly popped up to serve the demand. At first, they were straight clubs with straight Bounce artists. But New Orleans has always been on some different shit. For one, the audience was mainly women. It's always been that way—and it's probably why gay rappers were able to make it here. Gay and straight culture, even in the rap scene, has always been a little extra close compared to the rest of America. We're easier down here, a bit more open—about everything.

Addie was knowing every last one of these artists. He'd come over with new tapes and CDs and go on about them.

"Don't bring that here, Addie," Ms. V would say. "Gospel is God's music." It's funny looking back to that time, because while I was sneaking to the clubs with Addie, he was sneaking to church with me.

I met Katey Red in 1996, too. Addie had been telling me about this boy he met who dressed like a girl. "He's like you, Freddie," he said. "He's not afraid."

One Saturday afternoon me and Addie were going to a block party at the Melpomene projects, where Katey stayed. Just as I was zipping up my new white Nike tracksuit, Addie knocked on the door.

"Come on, bitch!" Addie said.

"Coming," I said, grabbing my red handbag off the counter and dabbing on some lip gloss.

"Look at you, girl," Addie said when I walked outside.

"You already know!" I belted out, in my singsongy way.

"You already know!" Addie repeated. As we approached the Melpomene, he pointed to a tall skinny guy in a little blue dress and long hair.

"That's Katey," Addie said.

"Addie, Addie!" she hollered. At six foot two, she was nearly my height. "Hi, I'm Kenyon."

"All right, Miss Kenyon girl!" I said, sizing her up. She looked fabulous. Me and Addie were feminine, but Katey dressed like a girl. I didn't know anyone at that time like that. She wore long natural hair, red lipstick, and blue eye shadow. She was standing with a very cute dark-skinned girl who she introduced as her cousin, Monney Mone.

"But you can call me Katey," Kenyon said. She talked fast, even by New Orleans standards, and I thought I detected a stutter.

"Yes, you can be a girl around me," I said.

"I love your hair," Katey said, zeroing in on the freshly trimmed bangs across my forehead. Katey and I just had chemistry. We were both gay boys in the hood, but it was more than that. She was sassy about her mouth so I knew she was gonna fit right in with me and Addie. We spent the rest of the party together. All day, Katey was spitting little riffs. She could rap.

After that party, me, Addie, Katey, and Monney became insepa-rable. We started hitting up the clubs and block parties left and right. We would stay out all night, shaking, twerking, and bounc-ing. It's what everyone was doing. Turned out Monney had a knack for words too. She was damn near a poet. I think she could have had a rap career too if she had wanted it. Both Katey and Monney would have input on some of the first songs I ever wrote.

One thing I noticed around this time was that Addie's frustra-tion went from talking shit to physical fights. I think hanging around me and Katey, who were both out and were able to embrace our gay sides, almost made it harder for Addie to be so repressed. His parents and uncle were so restrictive that he was truly terrified even to appear gay. It was so obvious that this sweet little kid was bursting at the seams to come out.

For real, I was starting to worry that Addie was gonna get popped. This one time me, Addie, and Katey went to this club called Pop's (owned by an older man named Pops) to see Magnolia Shorty. I had vaguely heard of this artist who was signed to Cash Money, but I had no idea just how special Shorty would turn out to be. She was one of the dopest emcees ever. Her song "Monkey on tha Dick" blew my mind. Her lyrics were a rare combination of hard-core, sexually explicit, and funny. At a time when rap was so serious everywhere else, only New Orleans could produce something so totally distinctive.

Me, Katey, and Addie sauntered in, like we always did, and got past the doorman no problem. But almost before we even got to the bar to order some drinks, Pops hobbled out from the back, leaning on his cane. He lifted it up and aimed the thing right at Addie.

"Adolph Briggs," he said, his arm shaking slightly, "you know you're too young to be in here. Your momma wouldn't be too pleased if I called her." Turned out, Pops knew Addie's mom from the neighborhood.

"Pops," Addie pleaded, crossing his arms over his chest, "I know, but there are lots of kids in here."

"He's with us," I said, trying to intercede. "He'll be okay."

"You've got one minute to get your ass out of here or I will call your momma and tell her to come get you!" Pops was now yelling. Suddenly, he lunged at Addie and grabbed hold of his arm. It was on: Addie tried to wrestle his arm out of Pops's hold. Pops's daughter ran over and a three-hundred-pound bouncer followed right behind her.

"Fuck you!" Addie snarled as the bouncer shuffled him toward the door. As me and Katey followed, I saw the bouncer lift Addie up and shove him out the door. Magnolia Shorty was gonna have to wait. "It's not fair, bitch!" I could hear Addie yelling from the sidewalk.

By the time me and Katey got outside, Addie was gone. Making my way home, I thought about my friend. So much angst in that boy.

I called Addie on the phone when I walked through the door. "Girl, you can't be acting a fool. One day someone is going to bust your ass and I won't be there to save you," I said. And I was serious. I understood that Addie's stepdad and uncle were riding him hard, but what I didn't realize then was that his defiance was a way for him to defend who he was.

Not too long after that, Addie came out of the closet. I pushed the issue, and I make no apologies for it, ya heard me? It happened one afternoon when I stopped by his house to see if he wanted get an ice cream. I did our usual call from the street. "Addie, Addie!" I hollered. He'd usually stick his head out his window. But that day, he didn't. His window was open slightly and I could hear Bone Thugs-n-Harmony's "Tha Crossroads" playing from his room. "Addie girl!" I yelled a little louder, and then belted a thundering "You already know!"

Addie finally appeared in the window. "Hush!" he said, his eyes narrowed and putting his finger up to his mouth. "Freddie, I got a girl in here!"

"Oh please, girl, who are you trying to fool?" I yelled back. Moments later, a young girl slipped out the front door. She just rolled her eyes at me and walked down the street.

Addie came out a few seconds later. I was prepared for him to be furious with me. I had outed him to his "girl." But he didn't say anything and we just started walking.

"You okay?" I asked.

"Yeah," Addie said.

"Sorry if I messed things up with your girl," I said, even though I wasn't.

"It's okay, " Addie said. "I didn't like her anyway."

"Addie, I told you, you a fag," I said.

"I know, Freddie," he said. From that point on, Addie was out. About a week later there was a knock at our door close to midnight.

It was Addie. "Can I stay with you the night, Ms. V?" he asked.

"Come on, baby," my momma said and let him in. We sat down at the table and Momma served us some Kool-Aid. Addie explained how he had told his mom and stepdad. "My momma said I was going to hell," he said, tears running down his face. "My daddy told me to get out." It hurt me to see Addie so deeply wounded. Ms. V walked over to Addie and hugged him for a long time. "You're perfect, Adolph Briggs. Just how the Lord made you," she declared. As tough as my momma could be, she always knew how to make you feel loved.

A couple of days later, Addie was allowed back in his house. After that, the policy there was "Don't ask, don't tell." Sometimes I think it was harder for him to live like that than it was when he was completely in the closet.

CHAPTER 9

THE ORIGINAL SISSY
KATEY RED

IN 1997, LOCAL RAPPERS like Juvenile, BG, and Master P were gaining momentum. They were grinding independently, selling tapes out of the trunks of their cars, and making a grip of money doing it. So goes the music business, when the majors get hip to bubbling scenes—and their potential for profits—they want in.

Soon enough, that's exactly what happened. I remember clear as day, the news was all over the newspapers and the city: Universal Records offered Cash Money a $30 million distribution deal. It was big news in our world—and in the music world, period—since up to that point, Cash Money had been a local phenomenon. But it was also an unprecedented deal because Cash Money could still act independently, retaining all its autonomy as a label. Universal simply helped it with the national distribution of CDs. At that point, southern rap—Miami, Atlanta, and Houston—was getting a foothold on the national hip-hop scene and that deal helped make New Orleans officially on par with the rest of the growing "Dirty South" phenomenon.

Just as Bounce was moving into the mainstream, in pranced Katey Red. I wasn't actually there the first night she got up onstage, but it happened in October 1998, and the event is legendary in New Orleans. It went something like this: Katey was with her friends—a group of dancers she called the Melp girls—at a Melpomene block party. DJ Lover Boy was spinning. Katey had a little too much vodka in her and one of the dancers egged her on to take the microphone. It wasn't the first time people had tried to get Katey to perform. We all used to try to get her to take the mic because she was always walking around spitting raps and rhymes—and she was tight!

"Bitch, I don't rap," she'd always say.

"You be rapping all day and night, bitch!" I'd respond.

At some point that night, she relented and took the mic. "Katey Red is a . . ." she shouted, leaving the sentence unfinished. The crowd responded: "Dick sucker!" Everyone started screaming and hollerin'. Katey kept going. "I'm a punk under pressure," and then, "when you're finished, put my money on the dresser."

People just went crazy for her. And by people, I mean the mostly female audience of Bounce. For women, the sexually explicit lyrics of Katey Red—and later, sissy rappers—resonated in a way that the typical misogynistic rap lyrics didn't. It was liberating for women to be the ones asserting these acts instead of being the target.

Katey could throw down, too. She was electrifying onstage and, after that night, every promoter in town was trying to book her. People were offering her five hundred dollars to perform a few songs. I remember thinking, *This bitch is getting paid!*

Katey never asked me to be her backup girl; it just happened one night at Club Stars. She was rapping onstage but her raps were more calls—that needed responses. She turned to me and sang, "Choir girl, choir girl."

I took the mic. "Ooh, ooh," I sang in my alto voice. Eventually it evolved into more. For example, she'd say, "Sissy Freddie is a . . ." and I'd say, "dick sucker." Or she'd say, "Katey," and I'd say, "Red." She'd say, "All them," and I'd say, "Heads." They were just off-the-cuff rhymes, but people loved them.

Katey's career went from zero to eighty in a few months. Suddenly, everyone was talking about the cross-dressing rapper. Two weeks later, Take Fo' Records offered Katey a deal. Just like that, gay rap was all the rage.

Soon Take Fo' started to book Katey for gigs out of town, in cities like Alexandria, Houma, and Hammond. There was also a demand for her at colleges around the state, like Southern University and A&M College. That was the beginning of spreading our sound outside New Orleans.

At some point we named ourselves "Big Freddie and K Ready" and played many bills under that name. Katey was extremely gracious to me during this time. She brought me on the road and would introduce me to the audience, "Hey, y'all, this is Big Freddie, show her the same love, please!" When it came time to record, she'd invite me to the studio to show me how she used to write, and show me how to work in the voice booth.

MY HISTORY-MAKING TWERK happened right around that time. It's significant because it really boosted my reputation as a shaker. But it also brought me together with Magnolia Shorty. My cousin Trisha and I were driving to a block party in her old white Buick. We pulled up at the party on the corner of Magnolia and Washington Streets when the light turned red. Waiting for the light to turn, I heard a dirty old beat blasting from the porch. I don't know what got to me, but suddenly I shot out of the car, bent over, and shook my ass on the back of the car like my life depended on it. The party was packed, and all them bitches went wild, clapping and screaming. When the light turned green, Trisha blew the horn, which got everyone more juiced. I jumped back in the car and we tore down the street.

My shake display became legendary. That night at the party, everyone was giving me props, high-fives, and bumps.

Later that week, me and Katey and Addie were eating lunch. "Everyone is asking, who was that big queen who was shaking?" Addie said. "And I tell 'em, girl, that was Freddie off of Josephine."

A few weeks later me, Monney, and Addie were at Detour when this girl with a round face and thin eyes approached me.

"Oh Miss Baaaayyyyy-beee," she said. "I saw how you shook at that block party the other day," she said, batting her eyes at me. Her enunciated way of speaking was melodic and I wanted to hear more.

"Yes, honey," I said, wondering who this woman was.

"You cut loose, Miss Baaaaayyyyyyy-bee," she repeated. "I loved it!" she added and walked off.

I was left standing with a huge grin on my face. "Who that?" I asked Addie.

"That's Magnolia Shorty!" said Addie.

"I love her," I said. After that, when I'd see Shorty I'd chat her up. She was a clown. She had such an endearing way of talking and a wonderful, kind presence about her. That girl loved the gays, and we loved her back.

CHAPTER 10
MEDICINE

IN LATE 1998, I got accepted to the University of Louisiana at Lafayette's nursing program. Lafayette is a couple of hours outside of New Orleans. My college stint was short-lived, but it's worth mentioning, mostly because I learned vital skills that came in extremely handy when my momma got sick.

I was torn about leaving home, since by then I was making at least some consistent money from shows. But my momma urged me. "You need a backup plan if that gospel career don't work out," she said. So I decided to go to school during the week and return to New Orleans on the weekends. I quit my job at Burger King and packed up some clothes, and Ms. V and Donald drove me to college. It was my first experience living away from my momma, and she cried the entire ride out to school. When we turned on to the campus roads and I thought about our looming good-bye, I broke down too.

Turned out, I actually liked the classes at UL Lafayette—I learned how to take vital signs, to do CPR, and administer shots. Caring for people came naturally to me and I still sometimes think, *If this Bounce thing doesn't work out, that's what I'll do with my life.*

Even though I liked what I was learning, ultimately, campus life wasn't for me. Raves were the "thing," and most of the white kids on campus were popping ecstasy pills and snorting coke. One thing I never cared for was hard drugs.

But I did start smoking weed, or, as I call it, my medicine. It was mostly because this pimply-faced hippie who lived in the dorm room next to me, Ralph, sold the most fantastic sticky green buds that smelled like skunk.

"Freddie, man, wanna come over for some herb?" he asked me one night. I was curious about this stuff that smelled like my mom's funny cigarettes. I watched as he rolled a joint. There was something entrancing in the way he trimmed and licked the edges of the paper. I liked it. He took some for himself, and then he offered some to me. I took a hit. The next thing I felt was a sense of calm I hadn't felt since being away at school. I was homesick as hell and smoke had a way of pulling the shade right over my loneliness. That night I started a practice of getting high that I still enjoy today. We all have our vices. I don't judge you if you want a beer or a martini—or a joint.

Meanwhile, back in New Orleans, the demand for shows was

picking up, and so were our appearance fees. Katey started pulling in $550 a show. Between block parties and clubs, we had gigs three or four times a week. I was making six hundred dollars a week, which was good money.

THE COMMUTE BETWEEN the city and Lafayette tore me up, so at the end of my first year at the university, I bailed. I missed my church and my family, so I packed up my suitcase and called Addie to come get me. I just showed up on my mom's doorstep one night.

"What are you doing here, baby?" she asked.

"Momma, I'm not going to finish school," I said. "I'm making good money here."

She looked at me and I could see a smile trying to peek out. "Okay," she said, opening the door to let me in. As I followed her into the kitchen, something felt amiss.

"Where's Donald?" I asked out of habit, scanning the fridge for any leftover red beans. She didn't answer. "Momma, where's Donald?" I repeated and looked at her.

"He moved out," she said, drying off some plates in the sink.

"Momma!" I said, getting up next to her and looking into her eyes. "What happened? Why didn't you tell me?"

"Just didn't work anymore," she said, putting away the plates. "It's okay, baby. God got me." Before I could ask her why she didn't call me or tell me at school, she said, "I'm going to give you his number, Freddie."

"Yeah, I don't know, Momma," I said.

"I know he was hard on you, but he did a lot for you kids, ya heard me? I want you to stay in touch."

"Okay," I said, unsure of how I really felt. I wasn't going to push it, but I wondered if she'd left him? Was it Donald's choice? He didn't exactly make my home life easy. But I knew Crystal loved him like a dad and I also knew Donald loved my momma once.

"Just worry about yourself, Freddie," she added. "You can't live here forever, baby, so you need to save some money."

"Right, Momma," I said.

MOMMA ALWAYS KEPT her feelings to herself, but it took me a minute to adjust to life without Donald. A couple days after getting home, I headed straight to Pressing Onward. I loved being back in the choir. One day, a rep from Gospel Soul Children, the crème de la crème of choirs, called and asked me to join them. This was huge. Gospel Soul Children was a world-class choir. They traveled the world, sang for government officials and city events, and released CDs. I gladly accepted and started to practice with them every week.

Looking back, I can see that this was one of the most crucial times of my life. Georgia and other church members were encouraging me to take my choir directing seriously. What they didn't know was that at the same time, people around town knew me as the booty-shaking Bounce rapper "Big Freddie." I was starting to understand that at some point I might have to choose between the church and Bounce. It was "All Hail to Jesus" by day and all hail to the ass by night.

ALL THE STRESS in my life at that time made me highly creative. I started decorating then, too. As with a lot of my talents, I discovered it by chance. My friend Marilyn from church was getting married but didn't have any money to decorate the reception. "That's no problem, I'll help you!" I said. I had seen Uncle Percy make something from nothing so many times. I went to Party City and bought a box of curly ribbons, a case of balloons, and centerpieces. I spent one week decorating umbrellas, decorating centerpieces, and blowing up tons of balloons. Baby, that room was decked out!

After that, I figured out that one way to make extra cash at the clubs was to decorate them for the night I had gigs. I started by telling the promoters that for an extra two fifty, I'd trick out the place too. They agreed and in no time, I was decorating Sam's, Escape, and Focus on the regular.

My business grew quickly because the clubs were showcases for my work. Girls would come in and ask, "Who did the decorations?" Before long, hos from every ward got wind of me and I was being asked to trick out all kinds of shindigs—birthdays, banquets, bachelorette parties. I'll never forget how one time this girl Colleen asked me to do a nasty party. Honey, I came with pink penis centerpieces and I hung dick banners from the ceiling. I even had a blow-up man and woman. I became known for my outlandish style and I was pulling in two hundred fifty to five hundred dollars a party.

CHAPTER 11
SISSY NOBBY

By 1999, WHEN I had just turned twenty-one, I was watching the Cash Money and No Limit record labels go massive on a national level. That year, more than half of the top-selling rap records were by New Orleans artists, including Master P, Silkk the Shocker, Mystikal, and the Hot Boys. Juvenile's album, *400 Degreez*, had gone four times platinum, which means four million records sold! It was a source of pride to see our artists—who had saturated the market locally for years—on top. Legitimately southern hip-hop was gracing covers of the *Source*, *Vibe*, and *XXL*.

Once a sound hits commercially, people start looking for the next new thing. Looking back, it's clear as day: when New Orleans rap blew up nationally, it left a vacuum locally. Sissy Bounce appeared right on time.

At that point, everyone wanted a piece of Katey. She was doing six or seven shows a week and I was on it backing her up. In March 1999, she released *Melpomene Block Party*, her first album. The cover art featured her in front of the New Orleans skyline with a bubble effect, so it looked wet. The day of the release, we had a gig at Club Detour and sold every single CD.

That night, curled up in bed, I devoured every word of text on that disc: liner notes, track listing, and acknowledgments. I was thrilled to be Katey's backup dancer and hype girl. But I couldn't help dreaming of one of these albums with my name on it.

After that night, I remember working on this song about sleeping with down-low guys, called "Ah Ha, Oh Yeah," with Monney and my friends Bookey and Trina.

I'd say: "Ah ha."

They'd say: "Oh yeah."

Me: "These hos."

They'd say: "They mad."

Me: "Your boys."

They'd say: "I had."

Me: "I made my cash."

I decided that I was going to record the song, so I called my boy who was a producer too, Law, and asked if we could roll through his studio on Rendon Street. He agreed and so me and the girls drove down there the next week and laid down the vocals to one of Law's hype Bounce beats. It was the first time I went to a studio without Katey and it felt good to be in charge.

The track was ready a few weeks later and I pressed up one hundred CDs. Back then it was low-tech, no artwork or anything—we just burned copies and I brought them to shows. I started performing the song at clubs and the crowd would go nuts for it. It spread quickly around the projects and parties and in no time everyone at the clubs knew all the lyrics. It was the first taste I'd have of something of my own, and I liked it.

Of course, once me and Katey started to pop, sissies started to come out of the woodwork: Vockah Redu, Chev off Da Ave, and SWA (Sissies with Attitude) all started copying us. But none of those bitches stood a chance, except this young punk Sissy Nobby, who was from uptown (Third and Galvez). My friend Anson was always hyping her up. "She kills it!" he'd say. "She is on fire!" But it wasn't just Anson. All the kids in the clubs and the promoters couldn't seem to get enough of her. I decided to find out what this bitch was all about.

In May, I was hosting cookouts with my mom on a regular basis for friends and family at my place on Josephine Street. I loved picking up a few pounds of crawfish, a dozen drumsticks, and some turkey necks from King's Market and throwing them on the grill on a Sunday afternoon. During one of these barbecues, Anson strolled in with this chunky little thing with short dreads. "This is Nobby," he said.

"How you doing?" I asked, slathering the corn with cayenne butter.

"Coolin'," he uttered in such a raspy voice, I thought either this queen had a gig the night before and strained her vocal cords or she was smoking five packs of cigarettes a day. But I smiled, offered her a soda. "I've been hearing good things about you," I said.

"Oh yeah?" she answered. She kept her eyes on the ground, maybe trying to hide a nervous tic, but there was something about her that was cute as hell. "Come to my show this weekend," Nobby uttered, staring off across the yard.

That weekend me and Katey decided to go see this Nobby at the Chat Room. Girl, she got up on that stage with her thick little self and flat brought it, you heard me? For the life of me, I cannot remember what songs she performed that night, but she twerked, shook, wiggled, and bounced till the crowd went wild. Her raps were well-crafted stories and her production was tight as hell. I remember thinking, *This bitch need a little refinement, but she's saucy and dope as hell.*

Her naturally raspy voice gave her a dance hall vibe. There was no question, that child was special. And Nobby was producing her own music, something me and Katey knew nothing about. She didn't have to rely on anybody for that hot beat. She was a one-girl show.

"Bring her over to my place," I said to Anson as I was getting ready to leave the club with Katey that night. "I wanna do some music together."

A couple of weeks later, I was counting my Benjamins—five of them, thank you very much—from decorating a church lady's party. I was figuring on treating Ms. V to a new cashmere sweater from Maison Blanche that she wanted, because all this time, she'd been supporting yours truly. This was the most I had ever made for a job, so I made up my mind to surprise her. I had "Bling Bling" blasting so loud rolling up to the house I thought it might blow out the windows. Who do you think were gracing my front steps? Ms. Nobby and Ms. Anson—I had completely forgotten they were coming, but I skipped up the stairs to them like I was right on time.

I threw my keys and the cash on the counter, like always, and Anson and I rambled out back to light up some smoke—couldn't be having it in Ms. V's crib. She smoked her funny cigarettes, but her children were not supposed to. I stuck my head inside the door and offered Nobby some, but she shook her head, already deep in thought, scratching out lyrics in a notebook and tapping her foot.

By the end of the night, Nobby and I had not only come up with some separate tracks, but together we were vibing off a song we wanted to call "Walk with a Dip." "Walk with a dip and you dip your hip" is when you are in the club and start feeling the music and can't help but sway your groin. We were riffing back and forth, *Ya walk wit a dip, and ya dip ya hip / Walk wit a dip, and ya dip ya hip*. I was excited about it because I knew the clubs were flat gonna eat it up.

It was midnight before I realized we hadn't eaten a thing. That's how lots of those sessions went. And I loved it: we were so focused on what we were doing, we lost track of time. I threw some red beans on the stove to heat and some turkey necks into the oven.

By the time we sat down to eat, it seemed like Nobby had finally relaxed. There was something lonely about her, but something sweet. She revealed that her mom and dad had both passed away and she didn't have any siblings. Poor Nobby had it rough. She needs a gay mom, I thought. But something told me to keep that thought to myself—at least for the time being.

About 2 a.m., it was time to wrap it up. I got Nobby's number and felt good about us working together. But more than that, I was glad I'd made a new friend.

After they left, I was so tired that my eyes were crossed, but Ms. V didn't like a dirty kitchen. So there was nothing to do but tackle the mess. I started to rinse the plates piled up in the sink. Something didn't feel right, but I couldn't put my finger on what it was. Then, I remembered: The money. The five hundred dollars. I had put it on the counter with my keys. *Where was my fucking money?* I snatched open every cabinet, searched every countertop, nook, crook, cranny. I crawled on the floor to see if it had slipped underneath the fridge or between things. No dough. Damn!

One thing about me: I am generous with my money, always have been, always will be. But I do *not* play with my money.

Even though I chilled with Anson all the time, I called him up outta bed. "Yo, my five hundred dollars is missing," I said. "It was on the kitchen counter. You take it?"

"Nah, man," Anson said.

"Well, your girl Nobby did then!" I slammed down the phone and called Nobby. Bypassing the usual hellos, I got straight to it. "You take that five hundred dollars off my kitchen counter, Nobby?"

"Bitch," she said, immediately over-the-top. "Why would I do that? Who the fuck do you think I am?" My gut has always been on point. I knew she had swiped it.

"You took it, girl. You know you did, and I know you did," I said.

"I don't need your money," she hissed. "I'm not no thief." And then, suddenly—*click*. Dial tone. Bitch hung the fuck up on me! I looked at the dead receiver and took several long, deep breaths. Finally, my pulse slowed as I recalled one of Momma's favorite sayings: "God has a way of making things right." I finished washing up the dishes and put out the light.

Working the clubs and decorating was keeping a steady cash flow, but I was starting to think about moving out on my own. For that, I would need some savings. I needed a part-time job, so I cruised down to the Middle Store, a convenience shop a few blocks from my momma's house, to see if they needed any help. The place was owned by this Iranian cat, Jamal, and I knew him from all my years buying candy and soda.

"I've got one shift," Jamal said. "Starts at midnight and ends at three a.m. You want them, they're yours." Overnight was perfect because I could do shows (they'd usually end by midnight, often well before) and still make graveyard shifts. Ms. V didn't love that I was working so late, but I assured her the store had a glass partition as security for the night shift. She was always proud of my work ethic. "You're like your mother," she'd say. "Always gotta work."

CHAPTER 12
BIG FREEDIA

IN NOVEMBER 2000, just as I was waking up after a shift at the Middle Store, Addie knocked on my door.

"What is it?" I asked, rubbing my eyes.

"Girl, some cute red boy in a Tempo is looking for you!" he said. "Saying some record label wants to sign you!"

"Who the hell could it be?" I said, stunned.

"Some light-skinned dude, a DJ. Said he'll come back around tomorrow."

Shit, this was the chance of a lifetime and now I had to wait all night. What if Addie heard the whole thing wrong? But I wasn't taking any chances. I wasn't leaving the house till I met this guy.

Next morning, I made a strong pot of chicory coffee and

planted my behind on the front stoop for hours. Sure enough, at about two in the afternoon, a little blue Ford Tempo came rolling down Josephine Street. It stopped in front of me. This light-skinned brother rolled down the window and asked, "You Big Freddie?"

"Yes, I am," I replied.

"I'm DJ Lil Man," he said, pulling over to the curb and getting out of the car. "My record company, Money Rules Entertainment, is interested in signing you." This was the first time I had ever been approached by a label, so I had no idea what to say. He passed me a card: "Kenneth Taylor is the boss. Give him a call."

Soon as he went around the corner, I walked back in the house and nearly had to sit on my hands to resist the urge to call him right away. Finally, about an hour later, I dialed Kenneth.

"You can call me KT," he said. "I want to meet you to talk about a deal. You interested?"

"Oh yes!" I said, not even trying to contain my excitement.

"Why don't you come over for dinner tomorrow night, and we'll discuss it," he said. "I'll pick you up at seven o'clock."

After we hung up, I called Addie to tell him the news. "I told you, Freddie," Addie said. "You're gonna do big things."

The next day, KT did indeed roll up in a fabulous old Toyota van with bright turquoise trim. The door opened and out came this very large man in khaki pants and a polo shirt. When I say large, baby, I'm talking like six hundred pounds!

"KT," he said, smiling, holding out his hand. His smile was warm and welcoming.

I had to force myself not to stare. "Very nice to meet you," I said, overwhelmed by the stark contrast of that baby face above the mighty girth.

"Let's go to my place," he said, waving me into his van. I couldn't believe this ride: velvet chairs, a TV, and a refrigerator inside! He was ballin' and I wanted in. On the way downtown, he explained that he and his partner, Stephen Michaels, were starting a label. We'd record at Stephen's studio across the river. *Studio? Record an album!?* I forced my mouth not to drop to the floor.

"Thing is, Freddie, you need to be your own artist," he said, pulling up to his house on Elysian Fields Avenue. "You can't back up Katey Red your whole life."

Katey gave me my start. I would be nowhere without her, so just thinking of splitting away from her put an ache in my stomach.

But God was sending KT to my door and it had to be for a reason. I also don't believe in coincidences. "I'd love to do my own thing," I said. I followed KT up the stairs toward the aroma of Cajun spices filling the doorway. His crib was sick: wall-to-wall snowy white carpets, leather sofa, and a huge TV.

"In here," he said leading me down the hall. "This is my studio." He pointed to an elaborate tape machine resting on his desk.

"Amazing," I said, scanning the masses of DVDs of movies like *Traffic, Gladiator,* and *X-Men* piled up on his desk. Hundreds of DVDs, CDs, and cassettes were stacked on the floor. KT's business was bootlegging the latest Bounce, R&B, gospel, and major motion pictures. He was a record store on wheels. Now I can look back and see the downside of bootlegging artists' work, but back then I was hungry and new and the only thing I could see was that he wanted me, that he was enterprising as hell, and that I could learn from this very large gentleman.

"Let's break bread," he said, leading me into the kitchen. He opened the oven to check on his corn bread. "I want you to be the first artist on Money Rules," he continued, serving us both plates of gumbo.

After we had finished, he looked into my eyes. "You interested in this deal, Freddie?"

"I am," I said, pouring some more gumbo in a bowl.

"I think we can make money together. I got a very cool producer I want you to meet. His name is BlaqNmilD."

And before I could say anything else he handed me a three- or four-page document. I tried to steady my trembling hand as I took it from him.

"I'll take a look and get it back to you as soon as possible," I said. I didn't even think of having a lawyer look it over. With us, nothing was done like that back then.

"Great," said KT, taking a bite of corn bread. "I'd like to release two songs to start: 'She Looked a Fool' and 'Rock That Ass.'"

"All right." I was going along with the whole thing.

As KT drove me home that night the breeze off Lake Pontchartrain was particularly sweet. I wanted to tell my mom and Addie. But I knew I had to call Katey first.

I was terrified. I knew Katey loved me as much I as loved her, but there was a lot on the line here—and sissies are as competitive as any other rappers, maybe more. I just came right out and told her that KT wanted to manage me and start pushing me as Big Freddie.

"Bitch, look at you!" she said. "Congratulations!"

A few days later KT picked me up in his van and we went to Sam's in the Ninth Ward. It was my first gig with a manager and I was beyond excited. I handed him the signed contract as I climbed in the van.

All my friends showed up—including Addie, Monney, and Katey. My dancers, the Josephine girls, and even my old friends Randy and Shaky B were there. When I walked out onstage for the first time alone, I was overwhelmed by fear. What if I suddenly couldn't speak? I swallowed hard and took a deep breath. As soon as I spotted Katey, Addie, and Monney, a calm came over me. I did "Gin in My System" and "She Looked a Fool." As I directed my dancers, I felt like this was my vision, my show. I was the conductor.

Afterward, everyone was hanging out backstage, smoking and talking, when Randy suddenly said, "Freddie is too masculine a name. What about Big Freed-a?"

I thought about it for a minute. It had a nice ring to it. From that point onward, I was Big Freedia.

CHAPTER 13
THE NEW CHURCH

I'VE ALWAYS BELIEVED that when people put their minds to it, they can change. One night, as I walked out of the club Focus, I saw this butch girl with braids standing on the street corner. She had that look, and I knew she was a dealer. But she had something else about her. Something that I liked.

"How much you charge to decorate my birthday?" she asked. I thought it might be some kind of hustle.

"When's your birthday?" I asked.

"January fifteenth," she said, which was the same month as mine.

"Honey, let's throw a party together."

"Hell yes!" she said excitedly, and then asked, "You need some weed?"

"No, baby—and you shouldn't be selling this stuff out here," I told her. I'm all for the ganja, but not the stuff off the streets. And young girls shouldn't be dealing like this, ya heard me? They can get in all kinds of trouble. "Give me your number," I said.

She read off her digits, and I put them right into my phone. When I rang her up the next day, I realized I hadn't even asked her name.

"Hello," she said.

"Hi, baby, it's Freedia," I said. "What's your name?"

"Kim," she said.

"Kim, what about a camouflage theme for the party? At club Sam's?" She agreed and the next day we drove to Party City together and bought green and brown balloons and streamers, camo plates, and napkins. I had Kim collect leaves and branches from along the street and the girl had amassed a forest by the end of the afternoon. The day of the party, Kim blew about a hundred balloons by mouth! She was a beast.

"You work hard, honey," I said. "You just gotta work at something honest."

"Can I work for you?"

I needed a hand with the decorating at that point. "Yes," I said. "You can be my assistant."

It took her a few months to trust that she didn't need to hustle, but she stopped dealing weed altogether after that. She worked as a waitress and helped keep my side business running. It was beautiful to see someone turn her life around and we have been best friends since then.

Watching what happened with Kim got me to thinking of

changes in my own life. I knew it wasn't going to be possible to sit in the pews on Sunday mornings after shaking my ass like a floozy the night before. One of them had to go.

I WAS TWENTY-TWO YEARS OLD when I made the decision to step away from Pressing Onward. It was one of the hardest choices I ever made, but I was signed to a record label now. KT wanted to record music and release albums. It was only a matter of time until Georgia and other church members got wind of Big Freedia.

Like church, Bounce gave me sense of connection. Shake your ass and your mind will follow. It had become my way of transmuting my pain into joy. For a generation of forgotten New Orleans youth, Bounce was the new church.

I got the courage to tell Georgia in the spring of 2000, right before Easter. We met at church to plan our holiday brunch and egg hunt for the children. Georgia was polishing the altar when I walked in. That smell brought me back to that first day when I was ten and Denise brought me to church. I thought back to the Easter brunches, the Valentine's Day fashion show, the Christmas Eve dinners, the voice lessons, and the church conferences.

I cleared my throat.

Georgia looked up, startled. "I didn't see you there," she said, giving me a bright smile.

"Grandma, I have something I need to tell you," I said.

"You know you can tell me anything, Freddie," she said, taking a seat on the choir stand and waving me over.

I sat down next to her. "I've been performing at clubs for months now," I said. "I'm a rapper."

"I know," Georgia said, resting her hand on my arm.

"You know?" I asked.

"Yes," she said. "Some kids at church told me."

"You've known all this time?"

"Yes, child," she said, smiling. "I hear you're good!"

"I want to give this a try," I said, looking down. "And that means leaving the church."

Georgia turned serious. "I'm gonna tell you something: being gay in that world will be tough."

"And that's just it. Me and Katey are changing that." I put my hands over my face, suddenly feeling self-doubt. "Do you think I'm crazy?"

Georgia smiled. "No, follow your gut, Freddie. You got something special."

She stood up and then said something that made me realize why I loved her so much. "You're always welcome back here at Pressing Onward, anytime you want to come back. I'm always here for you."

CHAPTER 14

THE WIGGLE BITCH BUS

SIGNING TO MONEY RULES and breaking out on my own only opened more opportunities for both me and Katey. We both had labels now, and we had agreed to work together to take this Bounce thing to the next level. As KT started booking me solo gigs, me and Katey were still in demand as a team, so a lot of times he'd book us both. Katey didn't have a manager, so she very much benefited from KT.

That year KT helped me put out my first single: "She Look a Fool." I remember going to KT's studio to record it. Going into the studio to record my own track was something I was still getting used to. But I was in command and I loved it.

In the meantime, I was becoming very close to KT. He became

a father figure, showing me the ropes of the music business. One of the very first lessons he taught me: "Always get your money before you hit the stage. Niggas never be around after the show." Up to that point, I had let Katey handle most of the money since they were her gigs. There were many nights where she was promised money after the show, only to find the promoter had bounced and was never to be found. Katey would get mad as hell. I wrote it off as part of the cost of doing business.

From the first show, KT demanded *all* the money from the club the minute we walked in. I'm not sure why it wouldn't have crossed my mind before, but back then there was a general understanding that you got half up front and half at the end. One night I had a gig at a club I will not name and when we walked into the venue and asked for the promoter, the bartender said, "He's not here. He'll be back by the end of the show."

"Tell him we'll be back when he gets here," KT responded and grabbed my arm.

"It's okay," I said, following him out. This was one of my first solo shows, and I didn't want piss anyone off. He just kept walking. When we got back into the bus, KT fired up the engine and started heading home.

"No, it's not okay Freedia," KT said. "No money, no show."

"But I dont mind, KT, for real. Even if I don't get paid."

KT slammed on the brakes and looked at me. "Don't ever say that, Freedia. Ever. You always gotta get paid."

"Okay," I said, nodding my head. Just then, KT's phone rang and wouldn't you know, the promoter had returned to the club.

"So you got our money?" asked KT. Pause. "We'll be right

back." That was just one of the many times KT proved to be right. We went back to the club and the promoter had the cash in his hand. He kept saying sorry for the misunderstanding as he forked it over to KT. To this day, I always get all my money up front.

BY LATE 2000, the competition between the sissies was starting to heat up. Sissy Bounce had taken over the club scene and all the little punks were jockeying for position. We were starting to clique up too. It went by neighborhood—me, Katey, Shaky B, Addie, Randy, and Desmond repped uptown versus the Tenth Ward punks— Sissy Baybe, Skittles, Dekey, Ms. Gettie, Kris, and Ms. Terry. Some healthy sparring is fun and to be expected, but in typical rap fashion, it turned ugly.

Everyone was after Katey mostly because she was on top, but even the other sissies hated on her. Punks were prejudiced too. All us sissies were straight-up gay boys. We have our dick and balls intact and like them that way. We dressed like B-boys (baggy jeans, Timbs, T-shirts) with some extra flair—earrings, purses, eyeliner. Not Katey. She wore heels and dresses. She was a transvestite.

On the Fourth of July, Katey's label, Take Fo', hosted a show at the Riverboat Hallelujah Concert Hall to celebrate her new album, *Melpomene Block Party*. The spot held about six hundred people. Katey had another show before this one, so she was coming later.

KT drove me, Addie, Shaky, and Sissy Baybe to the concert hall.

"You hear Sissy Raven fixin' to take out Katey?" Shaky B started talkin' smack before we even said hello.

"Settle down, bitches," I said. I knew Katey and Addie could be firecrackers, but with me and KT around, I didn't think much of it.

"I'm just sayin'," Shaky said, checking her lips in her compact.

"Just say nothing," I said.

The minute we got there, I scanned the crowd for old Cohen and Booker T. students.

Just then, Steve, an old friend from middle school, waved and started walking over to me, but before he could get to me, I was distracted by the sound of some ruckus. I looked in the direction of the noise and saw Sissy Raven and Sissy Baybe exchanging words. I couldn't hear what they were saying but they were rolling necks and hands were flailing. They were about to throw down.

I sped over, hoping Sissy Baybe would be able to extricate herself. "You gotta problem?" Sissy Raven said, rolling her neck.

Baybe ignored all I had said in the van. "What the fuck are you gonna do about it?" she responded, mocking Raven's neck roll. Then, out of nowhere, little Addie was sprinting toward them, with his arm cocked back. *Bam!* He straight-up punched Sissy Raven in the kisser. I remember clearly: Raven's tooth popped out and I saw it land on the ground. The rumble was on. People just started throwing punches and yelling, without even knowing why they were fighting.

"Get up, Addie!" I yelled. "Girl, get up!" But he was way past the point of being able to pull back. He had just lost it and was hitting anyone in his path.

Right then I saw this bitch Sissy Gettie start to pile on and go for Addie. My instincts kicked in. All I remember was that I swung around and smacked with my fist and she went down.

Next thing I knew, cops descended on us. Sad thing is that

Addie was so out of his mind, adrenaline surging, he didn't realize it was the police and started throwing punches at the cops. They got their clubs out and started pounding him. Finally one of the cops picked him up, and as Addie was thrashing his arms and legs in the air, the officer threw him down on the ground and cuffed him. By then Addie was screaming like a baby. I was terrified that he was hurt, but even more, I was afraid that he was going to get arrested. That girl wasn't gonna make it an hour in jail.

Addie locked eyes with me and said, "Bitch, why you didn't get my back?"

"I did!" I yelled at him. Now I was pissed. "I busted Sissy Gettie for you, bitch!"

"You're supposed to have my back!" he responded, as if he hadn't heard me. Addie was unstoppable, so I decided to talk to the police. Most kids couldn't talk to cops, but I knew you had to be respectful and calm and they usually listen. I begged them not to take Addie to jail. They agreed, and put him in the patrol car and said they were going to take him home.

"Thank you, Officers," I said, relieved that they took mercy on my friend. As the officers took off, Addie was in the backseat, his face right up on the window, tears running down his cheek. Katey arrived after the melee, and she did the show.

Waiting in the greenroom, I couldn't say if I was more mad or sad for Addie. He just don't know any other way but to fight.

Afterward me and Katey drove with KT to Addie's house. He came out holding an ice pack on his neck, his head hung low.

"Sorry, Freddie," he said, standing on the sidewalk. "I know you gave Gettie an ass whuppin'."

"It's okay," I said. "We're going to Club Michele's," I added and opened the van door. "Get in." Addie smiled and hopped into the van. We drove across to Michele's and I belted out, "Girl down!" Addie just started to cut up right there, in the van. Katey started riffing. The next I knew the van started to wiggle and wobble.

"It's the wiggle bitch bus," I said, grabbing hold of the armrest.

"The wiggle bitch bus!" Addie repeated, and we all howled with laughter.

"Settle down now, ya hear?" KT said. Through the rearview mirror I could see him trying to stifle his grin. That man put up with a lot from us punks.

From that point onward that's what we called KT's van. As we pulled up to Michele's that night, I could hear TLC's "No Scrubs" blaring out of the place. We walked in, lit up some smoke, and shook our asses all night.

CHAPTER 15
HOCKEY

"WHAT'S UP," I yawned from behind the glass partition one night at about 3 a.m. at the Middle Store. This kid set down chips, a Snickers, and a Big Shot pineapple cold drink on the counter and followed with a couple of dollar bills.

"Two ninety-eight," I said. He started searching his pockets for some change. I looked at his face for the first time. His hazel eyes were intense and his mouth slightly slack. I couldn't help but study the majestic wavy curls that framed his face. *Lawd, you cute*, I thought, suddenly perking up. He was patting the pocket of his Sean John button-down, coming up empty. "Don't worry, I got you," I said.

"That's what's up!" he said, flashing his huge smile. His lips were positively kissable. "Thank you!"

I had never been one to flirt. As a gay boy in the hood, I learned early that throwing game at another boy could get you a beatdown. But I was twenty-one and getting tired of being undercover. It was like I was out and everyone knew I was gay, but I was told not to be too flamboyant and my relationship status was ignored completely. Somehow, courage came over me, because I uttered, "You so cute," and then added: "Here, take this," as I slid him a note with my number.

"Cool, cool," he said, placing the piece of paper into his wallet and walking out the door. Right before the door shut, he turned around and said: "I'm Hasan, but call me Hockey. What's your name?"

"Freddie!" I closed that place down thinking of the boy who came in that night, with the cute fade haircut.

When I got home that morning, I had a little extra skip in my step. Every time my phone buzzed, I hoped it was Hockey. Finally, he called. We talked for hours. When I got off the phone, I realized my body had broken out in a sweat. I had about an hour to sleep before I had a decorating gig for a family down the street. Blowing up red and silver balloons, all I could think of was Hockey.

When I got home, I called him. "Come see me tonight," I said. By this point, my mom had started dating this man Keith. He was a postman and none of us liked him. It was just his attitude, like he thought he was too good for my momma's kids. But Momma liked him and that meant she spent a lot of nights away and it was just me, Crystal, and Adam. I had never had a guy come to my house. It was a bold move for me, but one I was ready to make.

"Okay," Hockey said. "Can you get my cab?"

"Sure, baby," I said, giving him my address. "Come down the back alley of the house tho', ya heard me?" I didn't want my neighbors to see him. He texted when he arrived. I ran down the back steps and paid the cabdriver. His curly ringlets looked gorgeous in the soft light coming off the moon. I led him into the backyard and we sat together on my futon and lit some herb. He explained that his family would kill him if they knew he was with a guy.

"I'm not gay, anyway," he said.

"It's all right," I said, touching his arm. Finally, he settled back on the pillows of the futon. I leaned in so close that I could almost taste his breath. "In fact, it's even better." I think it's because as a young kid, I was surrounded by straight boys, so they were the ones I had my first crushes on.

Sexuality in New Orleans isn't like any other place in the world. Straight boys sleep with men. And it's not down low or bisexuality. Some got girlfriends, some don't. People from the outside are always confused about that, but the thing is, when dealing with all the heavy shit—racism, drugs, and poverty—that we are slammed with here, sometimes we just have to let the minor titles roll off us. *Bisexuality* isn't a term I like and it's not one I'd give these guys, even though they've been with women. We call these guys trade boys. Ain't nothin' but a thang, ya heard me?

We made it into my bedroom and got to business. He leaned in and put his wet, glistening lips on mine. Hockey spent the next few hours introducing me to sexual positions I didn't know existed. He was younger than me, but way more experienced. That night awakened something in me. Before that, sex was forbidden. It was secretly feeling up red-skinned Joseph in his bed when we were supposed to be studying.

That night was the first time I cared for someone and felt it was reciprocated. And, though my momma sure wouldn't have approved of it in her house, the sex wasn't something I felt ashamed of. It felt intimate in a way I hadn't experienced before.

Over the next few months, I saw Hockey almost every day. If my mom was home, he'd come over for dinner and leave before bed. Ms. V was very strict about sex, didn't matter if you were straight or gay: "No one but me has sex under this roof," she'd say. If she wasn't coming home, I would sneak Hockey into the house. Crystal was the only one who knew the deal, so she'd let him in through the back door if I wasn't home from work yet.

But Hockey was adamant about not telling anyone about our relationship. He said he had cousins who would kill him. I reconciled being undercover because I was crazy for the guy. I hoped that, in time, he'd come around and so would his family.

One day in December, Hockey just straight-up vanished. I called him from work one night and left him a message. He didn't hit me back all night, which was very unlike him. After twenty-four hours, his phone started to go right to voice mail—and I started to worry. Three days passed and nothing, no word. I was starting to tear my hair out.

A few days later—and still not hearing from him—I summoned

the courage to walk to the projects and knock on some doors. "You know Hasan?" I asked some young kid passing me in the courtyard of the project.

"Hasan?" he said. "Nah." A woman walked by with a laundry basket under her arm and two kids behind her. My stomach felt like it might fall out. "You know Hasan?" I managed to get out. She just shook her head and grabbed the hand of one of her kids.

I don't remember feeling so profoundly despondent before. Part of it was that it was my first love. I had known longing and unrequited crushes, but this was love, which meant my heart was broken. I continued to call every few hours for the next couple of weeks, feeling like I was going insane, dialing over and over again, to no avail. Eventually the phone got turned off completely.

I don't know if I ever got over that bitch, but at some point in early 2003, the pain dissipated enough that I could start to move on.

And then came another heartbreak: Ms. V called to tell me that she heard that my beloved Granny Ruth had passed away. My whole body went numb. I had just seen her the month before and she was fine.

"How?" I asked.

"I don't know," Momma answered.

"When is the funeral?" I asked.

"It was last week yesterday, baby," she said. All of a sudden the numbness turned to rage.

"What? What do you mean?" I asked. I wouldn't think of missing Granny's service. "Why weren't we told?"

"I don't know, baby," Ms. V said. "I heard from Crystal's godmother, Cleo." Then she sucker-punched me: "Your daddy was there, too. He's out of jail."

"He was at the funeral?" I said. My head was spinning. My father was out of jail and didn't want to call his only child? And he didn't tell me that my grandmother died? It was all too much to take. I searched my drawer for a blunt and lit the fuck up.

Baby, I was on a heartbreak diet. After losing Hockey and my grandma, my appetite disappeared. Poof! Like that. I think I fell into a full-blown depression, but at the time, all I knew was that my body couldn't hold down food. I'd eat once in a while. Between red beans and rice and some corn, my stomach shrank, and I lost damn near forty pounds. Over the course of the next four months, my body transformed.

I never gained the weight back. Just like that, one day, I was no longer the fat sissy.

Just as I started to emerge from the haze of depression, something crazy happened. I was getting ready for a show at Detour. Uncle Percy had sewn studs up and down the front of this new Gap jean jacket for me. I brushed back my hair, applied some lip gloss, and walked over to the club. By the time I got there, there was already a line around the block. More and more nights were sold out.

I circulated through the crowd, waving to friends. "Hey, Freddie." This neighborhood kid, Ronald, was suddenly in front of me. "You need some smoke?"

"Nah, I'm good, baby, thank you," I said, and then as I stepped past him, I locked eyes across the room with a boy who looked exactly like Hockey. I thought my knees were going to buckle—and then in an instant, he disappeared. For a second I thought I could be hallucinating. I clinched my fists. I pushed through a group of girls, almost knocking one over, and started racing to the corner spot where I thought I saw him.

Suddenly Katey was in front of me. "What's up, girl?" she said. Seeing her jarred me back into reality. "Coolin', I'm fine," I said.

"I didn't ask how you was," Katey said and laughed.

"Okay," I said, smiling in an attempt to disguise my agitation. "See you in the back," I said and walked away. Addie and Monney were already there. I fired up a fat blunt and fell into a cloud of haze.

"You're up, Freddie!" I heard Addie yell and I put out the blunt and ran onstage.

When I got home that night, I felt my phone vibrating in my pocket. When I looked at the number, I recognized it. It was Hockey.

"Was that you? At the club?"

"Yes," he said.

"Where the fuck have you been?" I said, my hand shaking.

"Atlanta," he said.

"And you couldn't fucking call?" I said, trying not to cry.

"Sorry, Freddie," he said. "Me and my brother had to leave to go stay with family. It was sudden." Pause. "Can I come over?"

"Yeah," I said, my heart pounding with excitement. I had never felt so angry and overjoyed at the same time in my whole life. When I hung up, I suddenly burst out crying.

The sex that night was more passionate than I ever thought possible. All that emotion for six months was released. I held him close all night in bed, but I knew I could never trust him again.

CHAPTER 16
BLAZED UP

Exactly a year after my grandmother died, I got a call from a woman named Karen. "Hi, Freddie, I'm your daddy's wife," said the sweet-sounding voice on the other end of the line.

I was in bed, half-awake from a nap. I sat up and slipped on my robe. That familiar dread was in the pit of my stomach. "Wife?" I said, walking into the kitchen, flipping on the coffeemaker, and thinking, *Thanks for the invite to the wedding*. "I didn't know my dad was married."

"Me and your daddy got married a few months ago and this is the first I'm hearing that he has a son. I'd like to meet you."

I took out a cigarette and rummaged through some drawers for a lighter. So much rushed through my mind, most of all, Why the fuck couldn't my dad call?

I guess there was a prolonged silence because then she said, "You there, Freddie?"

"Yes, I'm here," I said. My thoughts turned to what my momma had said about forgiveness. I wanted to be there, but I was heated. "Nah," I said in answer to Karen's desire to meet me. "He got out of jail and got married and he can't call me? I'm cool."

"Can I give you my number, in case you change your mind?" she asked.

"Sure," I said and scribbled her number down on a receipt I found on the counter.

I hung up the phone and threw on some sweats and a T-shirt. As I crossed town to my mom's, a million things raced through my mind, including all the occasions he missed: my school dances, cheering, high school graduation, college. When I punched the steering wheel hard, I was surprised by my own anger.

Ms. V wasn't home yet, so I went out back. I sat in a chair under the oak tree and lit a roach, hoping to get a little puff before Momma got home. Right as I was about to inhale, she popped her head outside. I threw the roach down and smashed it into the dirt.

Shit, I'm caught, I thought. She looked at my foot and then back at me. "Hang on, baby, I got something for you," she said and disappeared into the house. After a minute or so of silence, she called out, "Be right there!"

She came out, holding a closed fist. When she opened it, in her palm there was a bag of weed.

My eyes widened. I took it out of her hand.

"For me?" I asked.

"For us, baby," she said, pulling up a chair next to me. "Your momma been smoking." I knew all those years that she smoked those funny cigarettes and I had found a roach here and there, but not in a million years would I have thought we'd get high together.

"I'd rather have you smoke here with me, than out there in the streets," she said.

I fished in my purse for my lighter, held up the blunt for my momma, and fired it up. As she exhaled, I thought, *I'm getting blazed with my momma.*

But I needed to get real with my momma, so I told her about the call from Karen.

"He's married?" Momma asked, and then I felt horrible that I didn't consider it would hurt her to hear that the man she once loved had found a new wife.

"Sorry, Momma," I said.

She grabbed my chin and held it in her hand. "It's okay, baby. I think it would be good for you to see your daddy."

"But he's been out of jail and hasn't even tried to reach out."

"Maybe he doesn't know how to find you."

"Bullshit, Momma," I snapped.

"Holding on to all this anger is only going to poison you," she said. I knew Momma was right but I wasn't ready to forgive.

"Freddie, if you don't heal that wound, you'll carry it with you your whole life," Momma said, taking one last hit. She stood up and stretched her arms above her head. "Now, come inside and let's go eat," she said.

"I will in a minute." I gazed up at the night sky and thought about all those times in my daddy's truck. About the constant feeling of abandonment that haunted me my whole life. I still wondered what he had done to get put away. Maybe Ms. V was right. But I wasn't ready to forgive yet.

CHAPTER 17
BATTLE OF THE SISSIES

BY 2001, I was the hottest local act. I was performing every night of the week at different clubs, like the Focus in the Third Ward and Sam's on Erato Street. I even performed at high school talent shows—wherever they'd have me.

I would either host or rap or both. The events that really popped were the "Battles of the Sissies." We came up with the idea as a way to help promote the nights. And it worked. Me, Katey, and by then Nobby would challenge lesser-known sissies, like Vockah Redu and Chev off Da Ave, to friendly rap competitions. I was still a little salty at Nobby for the money situation, but she was becoming part of our crew. They were typical hip-hop battles: our crew against theirs, who had the hottest lyrics, who could top who.

The Focus could only hold about a hundred people. It got so crowded on my nights that people would have to wait outside and rotate in and out of the club. My friend Sims had this spot, Sam's Night Club, and he offered me my own night on Fridays. It was exactly between the Melpomene projects, where Katey grew up, and Josephine Street, where I was from. It was twice as big as the Focus, so it was the perfect spot to hold these battles. I wanted everyone to be able to come—and they did. Cars would be parked all along Erato Street for blocks on those nights.

Everything was going fine until Vockah Redu started to have it out for Katey. Vockah was a sissy with six-pack abs and not afraid to show them off. He was from the Magnolia projects, a pretty infamous and violent place, even for New Orleans. Around that time, he was makin' some noise, but not like me and Katey.

Regardless, the battles were supposed to be fun and generate promotions for the club nights and they were successful.

Then came the night at Sarah T. Reed High School in 2001. They had a skinny teacher named Ed. I had met him a few months before, while I was performing at a club. I was at the bar getting a cup of ice when he walked up and I spotted him. Gays at a club are easy to spot. He walked up to me and told me he really loved my shows. We talked for hours that night.

"I'm going to make you my gay son," he said.

"Would you do a concert at the school?" asked Ed that same night at the bar. "I'm trying to raise money for the school." He said he'd pay us and I was happy to do it.

We agreed to do a battle and we set the date for two weeks later. The battle would be me and Katey against Vockah Redu and

Chev off Da Ave. Ed said we would determine the winner by how the audience reacted, which sounded reasonable to me. What I didn't realize then was how serious the problem was with Vockah and Katey. Addie told me Vockah had been performing a song called "Fuck Katey Red."

I didn't really care, but when Katey heard about it, she was mad as hell. "I'm gonna kill that ho," she said one day sitting at her house, smoking some weed.

"Don't pay them any mind," I urged, but she meant business. Like I said, I never liked drama. I always try to stay out of that type of stuff, but Katey let insults get to her.

"Don't let them get to you," I said again. "They just jealous."

The battle was supposed to start at ten o'clock in the gymnasium, so me, Katey, and about twelve dancers got there at 10:30.

Vockah and his crew came through a few minutes later. He was wearing a baseball cap and carrying this big floppy shopping bag over his shoulder with cardboard popping out.

"Okay . . ." I said, looking at Katey, as Vockah walked by us. "What's this bitch up to?"

Chev walked in all decked out in sunglasses and a big gold chain. When he passed us, he didn't say hello either. It seemed too serious. I got a bad feeling, but I tried to focus on my rhymes.

Right before we were supposed to start, Ed flipped a coin to see who would go first. Being that I was his gay son, I gave him a wink, like, "We better go second." You never want to go first in a battle because you want to hear your competition and what they say, so you can strategize how to play them.

Lo and behold, we went second. Vockah and Chev walked onto

the stage, which was at one end of the auditorium. Back then, security there was a couple of older kids who had on red shirts who were supposed to help with crowd control. Vockah was still carrying that bag.

These hos got props! I'm thinkin'.

I was right. "Katey wear size eighty!" Vockah hollered as he held up a cardboard cutout of a big high-heel shoe. When Katey gets mad, she gets serious. Katey's eyes were about closed right then. The crowd roared. Next, Vockah took a cardboard turkey out of his bag. "Freedia, the turkey bowl eata!" At that point, everybody was laughing so hard they could barely stand up.

I started to sweat. They came hard. I looked at Katey.

"Don't worry about this bitch. I got this," she said. We made our way to the end of the gym. Katey started rappin'. As it turned out, she had made up a little rap and didn't tell anybody.

And when I catch yo mom in them hallways / I'm going to rub them strings on her bald head. I knew there was going to be trouble. The strings on her bald head referred to those few strands of hair left on his momma's head and that was cold. It was one thing to dis each other, but it was an unspoken rule with us: you don't talk about anyone's mom. The whole auditorium started screamin'. People looked like they was passin' out just on that line. We won right then and there.

Ed said Big Freedia and Katey won but before he got to the end of the sentence, Vockah and his crew started rushing the stage, pushing by Ed and heading right for Katey.

Being that Katey was my best friend, I had to have her back.

"Come on, bitch!" I heard myself saying. Before any of us could actually throw punches, the security kids got in the middle and broke it up. Poor Ed, he was begging everyone to calm down. People were just shoving past him.

"Come on, y'all." I pulled one of my dancers off one of theirs. I couldn't do this to Ed. Everyone seemed to just stop right then and disperse.

You went over the line, I thought as we walked out onto the street. "When did you come up with that?" I asked Katey.

"Bitch, I been thinkin' of it all week," she said.

"You came at her mom," I said. Katey just shook her head. As had happened with so many rap rivalries, Katey and Vockah's beef turned real.

A few months later, Chev was having her record release party at this spot, the Warehouse on Earhart Street. Her debut album, *Straight off Da Ave (A Sissy with Class)*, was coming out that week on the Kings Entertainment label. We got word that "Fuck Katey Red" was going to be on it, so I was worried that Chev was spoilin' for a real fight. But since I'm not the jealous type, I was happy for Chev. She was trying to come up like the rest of us. Between you and me, it was Katey I was worried about.

SWA—Sissies with Attitude—showed up that night. They were young punks named Perry, Skittles, Chris, and Deekie. They weren't really that good but that didn't stop them from trying. A few months earlier they had made up a song about me and Katey called "We're Comin for You." It was a typical hip-hop ploy: take down who is on top to get noticed. As usual, Katey got mad.

"I'm goin' to deal with them hos," she said.

"They can't touch us," I replied.

The night of the party, me, Katey, Nobby, and eight dancers piled into the KT's van.

"All aboard the Wiggle Bitch Bus!" I yelled and we prepared to drive out to the Warehouse.

"You know Chev is mad at you?" Nobby said as she climbed in the backseat.

"Why?" I asked, turning the ignition on and throwing the last of my weed into my purse.

"Cuz the only way to get people to her party is to have you there," Nobby answered. Even if that were true, I still wanted to celebrate with Chev.

Before the battle even started, Skittles was throwin' slangs at us, talkin' shit.

"Bitch, you buckin' up, you betta want to fight," he mumbled under his breath as we walked past him. I just ignored him, but Katey got right up in his face. "SWA, Sissies with AIDS!"

Katey and I performed together that night. We did "Gin in My System."

I got that gin in my system / Somebody's gonna be my victim.

Then we did "She Looks a Fool." The crowd went wild. From the stage, I spotted Chev. He was huddled with his crew and they were heated. As I left the stage, the crowd was screaming, "Freedia! Freedia!" Nobby was right. I was outshining Chev at his own release party—and you never want to do that.

Katey was already waiting on the side of the stage for me. We were making about five to six hundred dollars a night back then, which was good money for us.

"Let's go," Katey said. Nobby and the rest of the dancers walked outside, but before we got to the van, Skittles and his crew were circling us.

These bitches wanna fight, I thought as I lit a cigarette.

"Look at this queen with all that makeup on her face," Skittles said, talking about Katey.

"You all got something to say?" I said. You could hear crickets right then. Nobody moved. "Like I said, you all got something you wanna say?" I asked again, as I unlocked the van door.

"No one is talking to you, Freedia," Skittles said. "Go ahead about your business."

One by one we packed in. From the backseat I scanned the van to make sure everyone was there but I didn't see Nobby.

"Where Nobby at?" I asked. Before anyone could answer, I looked out the window and saw that Skittles, Perry, and a gang of others were on top of Nobby, rolling around on the street. "They jumpin' Nobby! They jumpin' Nobby!" I yelled. Everyone jumped out of the van. Katey grabbed Perry and started swinging. I wrestled Nobby free from Skittles, and Nobby staggered toward the van. I stepped on some broken pieces of glass. When I looked at the ground, I saw fresh blood spots but hoped they had been there from before.

Nobby was hollering and covering his face, but no one could understand what he was saying. He slid into the backseat, still covering his face.

I climbed in beside him. "Nobby's bleeding!" one of the girls shrieked. That's when all hell broke loose. It was true, blood was spraying out all over the upholstery of KT's van. I was drenched in blood. The TV and curtains had blood on them. "They cut my eye!" Nobby wailed. "Those bitches got my eye!" Oh Lord, I thought. They had cut Nobby with that bottle.

That's when I climbed into the driver's seat.

"Tie this around his head," I said, throwing my towel to Katey. My hands were shaking so bad I could hardly turn the key. I sped off to the nearest hospital, University Hospital, on Tulane Avenue. I was running red lights and stop signs the whole way, all the while keeping my eyes out for cops.

"It's gonna be okay," Katey said, holding Nobby's head up. "You gonna be okay." Nobby just kept crying.

We all had to carry Nobby into the emergency room, which wasn't easy because that girl has some weight on her. The nurses came around the desk and rushed him to the back but by then, I think he was already unconscious.

None of us even talked in the waiting room. *Lord, help this boy,* I prayed.

Around 4 a.m., the doctor came out. He said it was a good thing we got there when we did because if Nobby had lost any more blood, he would have died.

"We saved the eye, but he won't ever see out of it again," he added. Wow, this shit is serious. That night, I made a promise to myself and to God not to engage in drama. I also asked Nobby to be my gay son. He needed my help, this boy.

"That was meant for me," Katey said. "That was supposed to be my eye."

While we waited for Nobby to get bandaged and released, the police arrived and interviewed all of us. We told them that it was

Skittles, since we'd all seen it with our own eyes. I never understood why, but he didn't get charged for anything.

Nobby's eye didn't heal properly and so a year later, the doctors had to remove it completely and put in a glass eye. The funny thing is, Nobby and Skittles are cool now. When they see each other out, they say hi and talk.

Skittles, however, did go to jail eventually because he wasn't done with Katey. A few months later, he pulled a crew together and showed up at Katey's house. Katey knew better than to call me, especially after my swearing off drama, so she called our other best friend, Adolph.

By the time Addie got there, it turned into one big gang war. Skittles cut Katey's right hand with a beer bottle and Perry cut her left arm. After the fight no one could drive, so they called me. I drove over there and took Katey to the doctor. She had to have sixteen stitches in her hand and she pressed charges and sent Skittles's ass to jail for six months for aggravated assault. After that, just like with Nobby, Katey made Skittles her gay son, because in New Orleans, no one holds a grudge for too long.

LEFT: Ross family portrait day, 1992—Crystal, me, and Little Adam (looking fierce!) standing around Mama V.

RIGHT: I looked an awful lot like Ms. V at nine years old! Here I am in 1987, posing for my third grade school picture.

LEFT: Sporting my Looney Tunes shirt and my Money Rules chain in 1999. I've come a long way style-wise.

ABOVE: The only picture I have of Pressing Onward Church choir. I'm the fat guy in the middle, 1997.

RIGHT: My favorite photo of my momma at beauty school, 1982.

Cohen Sr. High School
ROTC Ball — April 3, 1993

LEFT: Antoinette and me looking sharp at the ROTC ball, sophomore year of high school, 1993.

C.G. Woodson Middle School
Spring Dance — May 25, 1992

LEFT: I was fourteen years old here, posing for the spring dance with Zonitha, Shatara, and Angel, 1992.

ABOVE: One of my proudest days: Walter Cohen High School graduation in 1996.

LEFT: Halloween 2004. This was the first time I went out after being shot, and I dressed up as a mummy so the cast would blend in with my costume.

LEFT: Me, the fabulous Uncle Percy, and my gay mom Mark Tavia. This was our first decorating event together in 2002.

RIGHT: My first manager KT and me in 2001.

BELOW: One of my favorite performance shots at Echoplex in L.A. in 2012.

ABOVE: Devon and me at Club Caesar's in 2008, a year after we met.

RIGHT: My babies, Rita and Sensation.

LEFT: My sister Crystal, my brother Adam, and me getting ready to party in 2012 at Club Envy.

RIGHT: One of the last times Ms. V would go to Caesar's to see me perform, January 2014.

LEFT: The horse and buggy at Ms. V's funeral, April 2014.

Photo by Beto Lopez 2014

ABOVE: My current shake team and DJ. From left to right: Flash, Re Re, Skip, Tootie, and DJ Juan.

RIGHT: A selfie I took with my idol Beyoncé at her mother's birthday party in New Orleans in 2014.

LEFT: The original crew—me, Addie, and Katey at Katey Red's birthday party at Club Siberia, 2013.

ABOVE: My dad Freddie Ross Sr. and me on the set of *God Save the Queen Diva* in January 2015.

ABOVE: Boss and me at Club Encore on February 1, 2015, at my "all-white" birthday bash.

LEFT: Dancers Steph and Tootie with me in 2014.

RIGHT: Tootie and Steph in New York City in September of 2013 when we set the Guinness World Record for longest twerk!

CHAPTER 18
COMMERCIAL BREAK

I CREDIT MY MOM for coining the name "Queen Diva" sometime in 2002. It happened because she started a "social and pleasure club" with eight of her lady friends. They called themselves the Divas. They would throw parties, charity events, and other gatherings every month. I was the club's coordinator, which meant I decorated all the events. One day, my momma just called me the Queen Diva.

And so it was. I was Big Freedia the Queen Diva. The timing was perfect because in early 2003, my first double disc came out, which I named *Queen Diva*. Peaches was the first record store to stock it. I'll never forget seeing it on the shelf, in the Bounce section. The artwork was a photo of me in front of this Atlanta mansion surrounded by Greek columns. It contained twenty-eight songs, including "Walk with a Dip."

A couple of days after it dropped, Nobby called me fuming. "Bitch, you stole my song!" she said.

"Bitch, you stole my money," I answered.

BY THE END OF THAT YEAR, I was at the clubs five nights per week, which for me meant there were still two nights left to fill. That's when me and Katey came up with this idea for a "female impersonator" night, which we later named "Commercial Break." It was a mix of rap and drag and catered to the same straight audience as our regular sissy shows.

This was an easy sell because New Orleans has a long tradition with drag dating back to the 1950s and '60s with R&B singers and entertainers like Bobby Marchan and Patsy Vidalia. Both were signed to major record labels and were popular with blacks in New Orleans.

By the eighties, the scene had kinda died down, so me and Katey wanted to put our spin on it. Since I wasn't a drag artist, I was the emcee of the night. Katey would perform with two other girls. The first was Ms. Magnolia from the Magnolia projects, who was my friend Desmond. She was always coming with her fashion-forward gowns. Next was T-Money. She was one of my dancers, but she was extra. She had butt and boob implants. She was actually transitioning from a male to female. Like at the Sissy Bounce nights, all the different neighborhoods were represented: Magnolia, Melpomene, and me from Josephine.

I was excited to have Addie involved, so I called to tell him about our idea and to see if he was game. "Freddie," he said, all serious, "I met a guy. He lives in Lafayette and I think I'm in love."

"Look at you," I said. "You have a boyfriend!"

"Yes, Freddie, and he treats me right," Addie said. I was happy for him. Of all the people I knew, Addie deserved to meet someone who appreciated him.

Addie fell hard. For the next few years we didn't see him at all, so me and Katey carried on with Commercial Break nights without him. We started on Wednesdays at Sam's, since I knew the owner and he knew I would bring in the crowd. Each sissy would choose a musician to impersonate. At that time, everyone wanted to be Mariah Carey, Beyoncé, Monica, or Brandy. Each queen would pick two songs and every one of them tried to outdo the next.

They'd arrive early and bring CDs with the tracks they were using. I would determine the order and who was going to perform what. Each queen got fifty dollars a night and could take whatever else they made in tips. The bolder the queen, the more the crowd loved them and the more dollar bills were thrown.

"Bring it to the stage, my good friend, my good sister, Katey Red!" I would start off the night. It was really about who could inhabit the singer best—the gestures, the attitude, the persona. Between each of the performances, I'd call out, "Commercial break!" and that was the cue for the girls in the audience to grab the wall or a chair and shake their asses. It was also my chance to do my own material—"Gin in My System," "Rock That Ass," "Walk with a Dip." Lawd, the crowd would go crazy for those five minutes.

T-Money was the most out-there of the queens. She was as

close to a woman as you can be. She also came the hardest. I'd say, "Bringin' to the stage, the wonderful, the fabulous, the looking like a woman, T-Money!" She would strip down to these Lil' Kim–like tassels over her titties and diamond underwear over her genital area. "Looks like she has a pussy!" someone from the audience yelled and everyone howled with laugher. What they didn't know was that T-Money taped her balls to her ass crack every night with duct tape.

This one night T-Money had a shocking wardrobe malfunction. She sashayed onstage as Beyoncé, belting "Crazy in Love," filled the speakers. She threw down, *Got me looking so crazy right now, your love's got me looking so crazy right now (in love)*. She was feeling herself and everyone else was too. She kicked up her leg and flipped over a chair and while her legs were spread, one of her nuts popped out. She paused for a second. Just as someone let out a scream, T-Money rolled on the floor and jumped up with a kick. It was raining dollar bills on that stage—fives, tens, I think I saw a couple of twenties. I think she made like five hundred dollars that night.

The hardest part of my job was keeping these bitches from pulling each other's weaves out. The competition for songs was crucial, since certain tracks—Brandy and Monica's "The Boy Is Mine" and Beyoncé's "Crazy in Love"—made a lot of dough. One night T-Money came backstage before the show and said she was gonna do Mariah Carey's "You Will Always Be My Baby."

"You did that song last week!" Ms. Magnolia said. "I was planning to do that song tonight."

"Ho, I already claimed it!" T-Money said. "And it don't matter how many times I performed it."

"Settle down, bitches," I said. "T-Money can do it this week, Ms. Magnolia next week." They'd have a beef for a few hours, but they always made up by the end of the night. Those shows were fun as hell. The night got so popular that in no time we brought it to clubs like Streamline, Focus, and Detour.

CHAPTER 19

POPPED

IN EARLY 2004, I decided to move out of my place on the West Bank, and I asked Uncle Percy to move in with me. We found a small place on General Pershing Street in uptown. One thing about being poor: we take each other in when we can. It didn't matter that Percy was much older than me and not an uncle by blood. He was family at that point, and my momma and I were always going to look out for him. He helped me too, minding my stuff when I went on the road and watching over my things at night when I was out working.

On a Sunday in July 2004, I was leaving Club Detour when a friend who danced for me many times, Toya, asked me for a ride home. She was part of the Lafitte Girls (from the Lafitte projects), and she lived right down the street.

"Sure, honey," I said, as she followed me out of the club. I lit up a cigarette as we made our way to Uncle Percy's red Nissan.

"You tore it up tonight," Toya said.

"Thanks, baby," I said.

As we pulled into the driveway of Lafitte, Toya turned to me and put her hand on my shoulder. "Bye, Momma," she said and slipped out of the truck.

"Good night, baby," I said, rolling down my window and tossing my cigarette. I watched as she got to her apartment and shut the door the behind her. Suddenly, a young kid standing in the middle of the driveway startled me. My headlights shined right into his light hazel eyes and gigantic pupils. His white tank top was ripped on the shoulder. I recognized him from Detour. He didn't move, so I waited, figuring he was going to ask for some cash. When he started to come around to the driver's side of my truck, I thought he was letting me pass.

Next thing I know, a deafening *bang!* sounded so loud that I flinched. I actually thought the shots were coming from the projects, until the back window of my truck was struck and shattered into a million pieces. This fuckin' boy was shooting at me. Then—*bang!* I heard another. And another.

My instincts finally kicked in: I hit the gas hard and went into reverse. I kept one hand on the steering wheel and put up my right hand to shield my head. That's when the bullet struck my arm, right above my elbow. My body went into shock, because I didn't feel a thing. I sideswiped a parked car in the driveway and kept going. When I got the car facing in the right direction, I tore down the street at full speed and somehow managed to dial my mom on my cell phone.

"I've been shot!" I screamed, checking the rearview mirror every couple of seconds, blowing right through stop signs.

"Where are you?" she was yelling into the phone.

"Lafitte projects," I said, the adrenaline racing through me. "I'm going to the hospital." Right then, I spotted the flashing lights of a New Orleans police cruiser a few feet ahead making a routine traffic stop, so I pulled to the side of the road. I slammed on the brakes and jumped out of the truck.

"I've been shot!" I screamed, blood gushing all over my shirt and my arms. Suddenly everything went black.

Next thing I remember, I woke up in the hospital. And here's where it gets crazy: I was in the *waiting room* with my mom and a handful of other people waiting to be seen. My mom had wrapped a towel around my arm, and I was in excruciating pain.

"Why are we in the waiting room?" I asked, as I saw a woman covering her child's eyes from my bloody arm.

"The nurse said if it ain't life threatening, we have to wait." That's New Orleans: a shot in the arm wasn't high enough priority, baby. It took them over an hour, but they eventually put me on a gurney and wheeled me back for surgery. When I woke up, I felt sick to my stomach from the anesthesia, but at that point I was happy just to be alive.

A nurse was standing over me, checking my intravenous tube. Ms. V and Crystal were standing on the other side of my bed.

"How you feelin'?" the nurse asked.

"Pretty bad," I said, looking over at the boy lying in a bed next to me, sleeping.

"Surgery went well," she said. "The bullet is still in your arm."

"What?" I looked at my mom and temporarily forgot the pain. "The bullet is still in me?"

"Yes. When it doesn't threaten a vein," the nurse said, "they leave it in. The doctor will be here soon and he will explain everything." She smiled and walked over to check my roommate.

"Who did this?" Ms. V leaned over the bed and asked.

"Momma, I don't know," I said. "Some kid. I've seen him before. He was on drugs."

"You had a problem with him?" she asked.

"No, I didn't even know him like that."

"I'm gonna get that mothafucka!" she said, pursing her lips. I just wanted to rest. At some point, I realized that I recognized the kid next to me from the clubs. He didn't have any visitors.

"You okay?" I asked.

"Yeah, I got shot last night, too," he said, pointing to his foot. He waited a minute, "You Big Freedia?"

"Yes," I said.

"I've seen you before," he said. "I like your show. I'm David."

"How'd you get shot?" I asked.

"Coming out of my house," he said. "Don't know who did it." We traded stories like we were talking about where we got sweaters on sale.

The doctor finally came in and explained to me that removing the bullet could cause nerve damage so it was best to leave the slug in my arm.

"God," I said. "This thing is going to be in me the rest of my life?"

"Yes, you'll be okay," said the doctor. "Trust me, it's better than having the surgery."

David looked over at me. "I know who shot you," he said.

"Yeah?" I asked.

"I called my people. The kid's name is Shawn. He's from the Ninth Ward and he's been going around town bragging that he shot Big Freedia."

I was too tired to feel anger right then or any other emotion, for that matter. My brain was exhausted. My arm was throbbing so I rolled over and went to sleep.

The next morning, the drugs had worn off, and I was riled up. New Orleans is a small city and I knew everyone in every ward. I got my people on it. I dialed Kim, KT, and Addie and told them to be on the lookout for this kid Shawn from the Ninth Ward.

The next day, my momma came to the hospital to help me pack up my stuff.

"Take care, David, ya hear?" I said, walking over to him and holding out my hand.

"I'm getting out tomorrow," he said. "I'll come to a show soon." It broke my heart that no one came to see him the whole time we were there.

Me and Momma got into the car. "Boy, you better press charges on this kid," Ms. V said. She continued, shaking her head the whole time: "I'm gonna find out who his momma is and have a talk with her."

The second we walked in the door of my house, Hockey called.

"Yo, Freedie," he said excitedly.

"What?"

"The boy who shot you," he said. "He pistol-whipped his girl-friend last night. Police got him and locked him up."

God sure works in mysterious ways. I don't know for how long, or if he's still there, but that kid went away and that took care of pressing charges.

About a week after I got out of the hospital, I heard some guys had slashed David's tires while he was inside the courthouse testifying as a witness to a shooting. They waited for him to come out, and when he started to change the flats, they sprayed him with bullets. It's crucial down here.

I grew up with death all around me, but getting shot in the arm was the first time I felt like I sensed my own mortality and it had me shook. The physical effects were one thing; like when it gets cold, my arm stings like hell. But the mental effects shattered me to the core.

When I returned home, I was a mess. First, I couldn't sleep. I would wake up in the middle of the night in a cold sweat. After about a week of rest, I was finally healed enough to go to the gro-cery store. I walked out onto General Pershing Street, and my heart started to beat wildly. Suddenly I was gasping for air. I ran back into my house. I couldn't leave the house after that.

Uncle Percy was a godsend. He would get the groceries and cook meals for me. Friends and family picked up the slack. Kim came over and cooked fried chicken and corn. Crystal would check on me every few days, always asking me what I needed from the outside world. Hockey did my laundry, picked up my weed, and ran all my errands.

Of course, if I couldn't leave my house, I wasn't going to the clubs, which meant I wasn't bringing in one dime. I had $543 in my bank account. I tried everything to will myself out of the house, but I would get that fight-or-flight sensation every time I stepped out. I was fully agoraphobic.

"You cannot be captive in your own house, baby," my mom told me on the phone one day. "You need to get over it."

Of course, but how? I wondered.

This went on for a few months and I started to fall into despair. I didn't open the shades or clean for weeks at a time. My apartment started to resemble how I felt.

A FEW WEEKS before Halloween of that year, KT called to tell me that he was going to have surgery at Tulane Medical Center for his sleep apnea. It was giving him such trouble, but with his weight, I worried about him. When I hung up the phone, I felt a pang of guilt, knowing I probably wouldn't be able to get out of the house to visit him.

Turned out I was right to worry. Two days after the surgery KT's son, Ken, called me.

"KT died," he said, his voice trembling.

"What?" I said in shock. "What happened?"

"He collapsed on the floor when he got up to go to the bathroom. When the nurses found him, they couldn't lift him up on the operating table in time. He had a heart attack."

"Oh God," I said. "I'm sorry, Ken." I was stunned. I was numb. KT was the first one to believe in me, and I felt disgusted that I didn't see him in the hospital. All because I couldn't get the fuck out of my house.

I curled up on my couch and cried.

The funeral was the following week. A few days before, I drove to a flower shop and picked out the most gorgeous carnations, lilies, and a wreath.

When I walked into my apartment, Uncle Percy was sitting on the couch. "You left the house!" he said.

"Oh my God," I said, processing it all. I was so caught up in the planning of KT's funeral that I didn't even realize I had left my place. The next day I drove straight to Blessed Trinity Catholic Church with my two stand-up flower arrangements and wreaths packed into the back of Uncle Percy's truck, and I attended KT's funeral.

There wasn't a space available in the church when I arrived, but I managed to make my way into the front with everyone. All of KT's family and friends were there. KT was a loved man. Crazy, looking back at these times. It was filled with such joy and tragedy, all at the same time. That's how it is in New Orleans.

CHAPTER 20
RECONCILIATION

MY BRUSH WITH DEATH changed me. The thought that I could have died without seeing my dad didn't sit right with me. I dug up the receipt with the phone number and dialed my dad's wife, Karen. She invited me to their home in Norco, a few miles from where my grandparents had lived in St. Rose. I agreed to go the following weekend.

Getting ready that day to see my father after twenty-one years scared me to my core. The anger and confusion I felt toward him had been locked away for so long, I was terrified to face it. I was twenty-five now, and the last time I saw him I was four. I still didn't know the reason for his incarceration. Would I like his new wife? Shit, I was a gay Bounce rapper. Would he even want me for a son?

Scanning my closet, I finally decided on white pants, a brown shirt, and some matching brown boots. I wanted to look nice for him, but I wasn't ready to tell him that his son was one of the most well-known gay rappers in New Orleans.

Memories of my grandparents rushed back as I drove the road I had gone down so many times. Granny Ruth and all her food, the trips to Kart N Carry with my grandfather.

When I got to the house, I sat in the car for a moment, contemplating what I would say. There is no script for reuniting with an estranged dad after twenty-one years. Standing at the front door, a Curtis Mayfield song sounded from inside. I tucked some stray hairs back into my pompadour and knocked. A petite light-skinned woman with a warm smile and gorgeous blue eyes greeted me.

"I'm Karen," she said, and came out to hug me.

Behind her came my dad. His brown Kangol flat cap hung so low, it almost covered his face. When our eyes met, I actually gasped for air. He had the same smile and bright eyes that I remembered, but prison had hardened his face. For the first time in my life, I thought about what that must have been like for him, to be sitting in a cell for nearly twenty years, without his son.

The silence was almost unbearable. "Poopie," he finally said, opening his arms. As we embraced, I could feel his shoulders trembling. I couldn't hold back my tears either. In that moment, nothing mattered except that I was with my dad again.

"I missed you, Dad," I said, taking a step back but still hugging him for a minute.

"Me too, son," he said, slightly stilted. Then he managed to get out, "Are you doing okay?"

"Just fine, Dad," I said. We spent the next few hours catching up on our lives. Over a feast of gumbo and crawfish, I told him I was a choir singer and a decorator. He didn't ask if I was gay and I didn't offer up the information. Some people think that's crazy, but that's the way it is in my family. There's a lot of love and a lot of unspoken truths.

He told me he met Karen through his sister and that he was trying to rebuild his life.

I finally got the nerve to ask him what I had been wondering my whole life. "Why did you get locked up, Dad?"

"I wouldn't rat out a friend," he said. "That's all you need to know." Was it? I wanted to push it, but looking into his eyes I saw a defeated man, and one who wanted to make good. Maybe that was enough for me to know. I said nothing—and haven't since that day.

At the end of the night, Karen walked me to the door. As I stepped out onto the porch, she said, "Freddie, I love your daddy. I'm not trying to take your momma's place, but I consider you my family too."

I left that night feeling a calm I hadn't felt in a long time. All those years of being racked by indecision were over. I wasn't healed; I never will be. But I had taken a monumental step forward in making peace with my past.

CHAPTER 21
KATRINA

By THE SUMMER OF 2005, my life was almost back to normal. The physical wound from the bullet was almost healed. The anxiety about it was being managed. But mostly I felt an incredible relief from reconciling with my pops.

For some reason, though, I couldn't seem to get over being in my apartment. I had been a prisoner for so long that my bedroom, the walls—everything—reminded me of that dark time. I decided to move out. I was performing like mad, and by then I had so many wedding requests, I was actually turning them down. For the first time in my life, I had a bank account with more than a grand, because of all my gigs. Uncle Percy was game to move too, so we started to look for apartments that spring.

It was also hurricane season. When it comes time for storms in New Orleans, insurance agencies start trying to peddle renter's or flood insurance like crazy. I had never had it before, but when this man got me on the phone and explained the different policies, I thought, *Okay, maybe I should*, and I agreed to take out a policy that day over the phone. I told him I was thinking of moving and he explained that the insurance would roll over to my new place.

ONE DAY IN LATE JULY, I was at my mom's, visiting Crystal and the new baby, CeCe, when I came across an ad in the newspaper for a two-bedroom apartment on Painter Street in the Eighth Ward. I called the realtor. A woman answered the phone and said the place was unlocked, so Hockey and I drove out there together the next day.

As we turned onto Painter, I spotted a freshly painted white building about halfway down the gorgeous tree-lined street. Even better, it was the top-floor apartment of a duplex. The front door opened onto a long hallway that had brand-new white carpets. Baby, the kitchen had appliances that white people had: a dishwasher and a trash compactor! It also had not one but two refrigerators! At the very end of the apartment was a small sunroom, encased in great big windows, the kind of space I had dreamed of for all my cactus and ivory plants. The room also looked out on a magnificent oak tree that almost took my breath away. It must have stood sixty feet tall, and its gorgeous twisted branches came all the way up and over the house. I was so excited, I could hardly contain myself!

"You gotta take this," Hockey whispered. I dialed the real estate woman. She said it would be ready in the middle of August.

"I'll take it," I said, envisioning all the new ferns I could plant. Back in those days, no one ran credit, in part because there really wasn't much credit to be had. Anyway, I was known enough around town that some things were easier for me, like renting apartments and opening bank accounts. The realtor knew who Big Freedia was and was happy to give me the apartment.

When I picked up the keys a couple of weeks later, the agent mentioned that the downstairs tenants were gone for the summer, which would turn out to be a blessing on a few fronts: First, the night me and Uncle Percy moved in, we were so loud. Thankfully, Hockey helped us because we needed all the help we could get unpacking. We spent hours hauling furniture up the stairs. I asked Hockey to nail my collection of African masks to the wall in my bedroom while I hung my framed pictures of my family and my new African print tapestry in the living room. As we unloaded boxes into each room of the house, I turned up Juvenile's "Slow Motion," which was the summer anthem all over the country, not just in New Orleans.

Our first night in the place, me and Hockey cozied up on the sofa bed in the living room. Uncle Percy took the wingback chair. It was a typical sticky New Orleans summer night. I rolled up some weed and gazed out the window: The oak tree's limbs looked like giant arms protecting us. I watched the hot-pink sky as the sun set. It was a perfect night.

"You did good, Freddie," Hockey said, grabbing the smoke from my hand and puffing hard.

"Yes, baby," I said, leaning back and closing my eyes. My life seemed like it was falling into place, finally.

Over the next two weeks a couple of fortuitous things happened: First, Uncle Percy and I decided it was time for a cookdown, so we went to the grocery store and stocked up on food. We packed both refrigerators with meats, crawfish, shrimp, rice, grits, cheeses, potato chips, cereal, sodas, juices, and milk. I was going to invite the family and make my specialty—pasta jambalaya, smothered pork chops, and corn on the cob.

When we returned from the store that day, I checked my mailbox. It looked like that insurance policy check had already arrived. In hurricane zones like New Orleans, they get you the money before the storm hits. But I was too concerned with the crawfish to open it, so I jammed it into my back pocket and started to peel the shrimp.

Hockey was sitting in front of the TV transfixed by the news that a big storm was headed our way. Every channel and radio station was talking about a category 3 or 4—even 5—hurricane that was getting ready to hit the Gulf Coast.

"Momma, Adam, and Crystal are coming for dinner!" I yelled out to him from the kitchen.

"I'm gonna head home," he said.

"Stay," I said, and walked into the living room. He was already putting his Saints cap on and heading toward the door. I was so tired of living this secret life.

"You know I can't," he said. He kissed my cheek. As he walked out the door, I thought: I don't know how long I can do this.

I went to the kitchen and started splitting the shrimp shells. Peeling the skins off, I practically ripped the shrimps to shreds. My phone beeped, temporarily distracting me from my frustration. It was Ms. V.

"You heard the news?" she asked.

"Yes, Momma," I answered, stirring my roux. My mom had experienced Hurricane Betsy in 1965, a category 4 hurricane that devastated New Orleans. She was only five years old when it struck, but she and everyone who lived through it were traumatized.

"We need to get out of here," she said.

"Shit don't never happen," I responded. For the last storm, I'd left town, and the only thing that had happened was my place got robbed. Plus, I had just gone to the grocery store and the gray clouds didn't look any different from all the other times. There wasn't even much growl to the thunder.

"Don't be stupid!" she roared. "I'm going to Shreveport with Keith and you and Crystal and the baby better come, ya heard me?" Shreveport is in the northwestern corner of Louisiana, well inland from the Gulf of Mexico.

I sure wasn't going to go to the country to stay with Keith.

"I'll stock up on water and batteries and wait it out, like I always do," I told her.

"What the fuck are you talking about?" she yelled. "Baby, the mayor is ordering people to evacuate!"

Crystal, Adam, and the baby walked in just then. "Storm is coming," I said and looked at them. "You wanna go with Mom and

Keith or stay here?" Ms. V was mad as hell when I told her they wanted to stay with me.

"You kids don't listen!" she hissed, and slammed down the phone.

Crystal unwrapped CeCe from her blanket and let her down onto the new white rug. Strands of curly hair were starting to pop out of her head. She pulled herself up with all her might and started to crawl down the hallway.

"Come here, CeCe," I said. "Uncle Freddie wanna get a good look at you." I lifted her up in front of my face and stared into her beautiful brown eyes. She smiled back at me.

"Light the candles," I told Adam. Dinner was just about ready. Uncle Percy set four places with red paper plates and napkins on the dining table. I made my momma's recipe for jambalaya and, baby, the second it hit my mouth it set off a whirlwind of spicy flavors so delicious that I temporarily forgot about the impending storm. "You made enough to feed an army," Crystal said.

We kept the TV on through dinner. One of the last news reports to get through said if you haven't left New Orleans yet, Mayor Ray Nagin wants you to stay put.

The sun was setting as I finished off the last cob of corn. A big gust of wind blew into the kitchen and through the dining room, knocking down the candles. I grabbed them and put them into the kitchen sink. Then, suddenly the kitchen window slammed shut and CeCe started to cry.

"It's okay," Crystal said, turning CeCe over on her belly and rubbing her back. I went through the house to close all the windows. When I got to the sunroom, I saw a squirrel run down the trunk of that great oak tree, looking for cover.

The storm hit at about eleven o'clock that night. Rain pounded down on the house. A few hours later, the wind started to howl like a freight train. The lights and TV went out. I had a couple of bars on my phone, so I turned it off to conserve juice. I lit some candles and helped put Crystal and the baby to bed. They stayed on the sofa bed in the living room. Adam slept on the floor.

I climbed into my bed, put the pillow over my head, and tried to sleep. As I stared at the ceiling, thinking of Hockey, I was suddenly and violently jolted up by an ear-piercing, crackling sound. Then the whole house shook. What the fuck? I thought. Then I heard Crystal scream. I ran down the hallway to the living room.

"Fuck!" Adam yelled. "Fuck!" The oak tree had fallen through our sunroom and damn near cut the living room roof in half, missing Crystal and the baby by only a few feet. Oh God, this wasn't good. The wind was blowing into the living room and rain was coming down. It's strange the details you remember in a panic, but I recall seeing the lamp fall over and the paper napkins on the coffee table blowing across the room. I looked over at CeCe. She was sound asleep in Crystal's arms.

Uncle Percy came out in his robe. "Oh my God," he said, looking stunned.

"The tree damn near killed Crystal and Adam!" I said as I fished around for a flashlight. For the rest of the night, we all huddled together in my room. It took hours, but I finally fell asleep to the sound of Crystal crying.

A few hours later an even louder thunderous boom, an explosion, sounded from outside in the distance. We all sat up. Do I dare go to the window and look out? I thought. Do I use my precious cell phone juice to call my mom or 911? I walked over to the window and saw nothing. We would later find out that it was a barge hitting the levee and breaking it. But at the time we had no idea and it just felt like the apocalypse that the pastor used to talk about in church.

"Everything is okay," I said, trying to stay strong for them.

"I'm scared, Freddie," said Crystal, cradling CeCe to her chest.

"God got us," I said. *Lord, Ms. V was right*, but I kept that thought to myself.

The next morning, I woke up soaked in sweat. Except for the gigantic tree in our living room, everything seemed okay in the house. I would have laughed if I wasn't so damn hot. I went outside onto the street. The air was so thick, even by New Orleans standards, that I patted my head with the end of my T-shirt. All the trees on Painter Street were toppled over. Power lines covered the road and sidewalks. A kid pedaled by me on his bike.

"Watch out for the power lines, baby," I yelled, but he didn't even turn back or respond. I went back into the apartment and sat with Uncle Percy in the kitchen. "The storm done passed," he said.

"Thank God," I said, hoping that there was some power so I could call a crew to come fix the roof. When I went to shut the window in the living room, I saw something I'd never seen in my life: water pouring down the streets, steadily rising higher and higher. Looked like the goddamn Mississippi River was coming our way.

"Ohhh myyyy Gawwwwd," I said, drawing out each word. I could feel my shoulders tense up. "Come here, Percy," I said, waving him over. "Where's all this water coming from?" It wasn't stopping!

"God have mercy," he said, standing behind me. "The levees must have broke. That's what the news was saying yesterday, child, that the levees weren't strong enough." Then I remembered hearing about these levees and how they were old and at risk to break, but I never did take it too seriously. Here in New Orleans, everything is always about to break.

I called Crystal and Adam in from my bedroom. "We need to get to the roof," I said, remembering that I had left the tool chest in Percy's truck. I ran to the front door. As I opened it, water started to pour into the house, soaking the new white rug. Thank God the downstairs apartment was empty, because it was fully submerged in water. When I saw the water reach the top of my mom's Toyota Celica and the windows of Uncle Percy's truck, I knew we were in serious trouble.

I managed to find the hammer I had used to hang the photos. I pulled the attic ladder down and climbed into the attic and started beating the ceiling as hard as I could. When I got too tired, Adam took over. He was skinny, but strong as hell. While that was happening, Uncle Percy found some duct tape and spelled out "Four Adults One Child" on a white bedsheet.

Crystal was crouched in a corner, crying. "Freddie, what are we gonna do?" she asked.

"It's gonna be okay," I said.

"Got it!" yelled Adam, so Uncle Percy and I went up to the attic and sure enough, Adam had pounded a hole in the roof.

I told Crystal to stay in the house and me and Uncle Percy went to the roof. By the time we got there, there were tons of people on top of their homes too. Planes and helicopters were flying by. Uncle Percy and I held up the sheet. Directly across from us, a man and three young boys stood motionless. One of the boys was crying so hard, his brother grabbed his hand.

A helicopter suddenly came low, looking like it was heading toward us. Me and Uncle Percy waved the sheet in the air with all our might. It passed overhead and stopped at the apartment building at the very end of Painter Street. We watched as they rescued all those people one by one. When the crew was finished, we yelled at them to rescue us too, but the helicopter took off and the sound of the engine got fainter and fainter. As we all remained there silent, praying to hear the sound of the engine again, I realized it wasn't coming back.

I lit a cigarette. My hand was shaking. I got my phone out and turned it on. There was no service. Towers were down. The water was starting to smell like sewage. Were we going to make it? I envisioned my mom getting the news that all her kids had perished in the storm. The thought hit me in the gut. How was God going to judge me? I grabbed my stomach, thinking I was going to hurl.

"Hey!" A scream interrupted my thoughts, and I looked down into the water. It was the man from across the street with the kids, swimming toward me.

"You got any food?" he pleaded, as he tried to tread water. "I got kids in the house and they hungry."

"I got you," I said, then jumped down into the house, ran into the kitchen, and grabbed the wrapped turkey and ham from the re-frigerator. I just started tossing it out the window. Food was hitting the water and he was grabbing it.

"God bless you," he said. "Thank you!"

We remained in the house for two more days. Thankfully we had the food from the night of the storm, and enough formula for CeCe. Crystal asked every few hours if someone was coming to get us.

"Yes, child, of course," I'd answer, having no idea if that was true. One afternoon, I was waiting up on the roof and a man and woman came by in a motorboat already half filled with people. They were just folks from two blocks down the street who had a boat and were rescuing people on their own.

"How many you got?" the woman asked.

"Four," I said, "and a baby."

"Get in," she said. I gathered diapers, formula, blankets—anything I could for the baby. I ran to my closet and grabbed the first pair of shoes that I saw.

First I lifted CeCe and handed her to the man in the boat; then Crystal, Uncle Percy, Adam, and I got in. The boat brought us to Elysian Fields, which felt like heaven. The field was totally dry. There must have been a couple of hundred evacuees but there were no services, no police, and no drinking water, so we couldn't stay. Everyone was talking about heading to the 610 bridge, since it was above water, and that's where the buses were coming to move people out of town.

A group of people led by a man even taller than me started to walk.

"Come on," I said, and looked at Crystal, Adam, and Uncle Percy while slipping on my sneakers. When I got my feet inside them, I realized I had grabbed old shoes that were a size too small. There was no time to fuss, so I shoved my big-ass feet in them good, and we started walking. Gradually, the flood appeared again. First we were up to our ankles in water, then our waists, and then I was holding CeCe's diapers and formula above my head to keep them dry. For a second, I felt something on my leg in the water and I started kicking my foot. A piece of wood drifted to the surface. I didn't need an alligator or some snake in the water. A man paddled up to us in a rowboat and said he would take us in separate trips to the bridge. Kids and elderly went first, and he took us all to safe ground.

When we got to the bridge, a few hundred others were there too, waiting for these supposed buses to take us to the Superdome. We decided to walk to the St. Bernard exit, which was a good mile more. I took CeCe in my arms, and off we went.

"I can't walk anymore," Crystal said, planting herself on the ground.

"No, baby, come on," I said and lifted her up. "We have just a little ways to go." When we got to the St. Bernard exit, everyone was talking about how the school buses weren't coming. I realized we might be staying there for a good bit and I was going to have to prepare Crystal.

"We gonna sleep here, baby," I said. I found an edge of the bridge and laid my shirt and towel on the ground. Adam had a small scrap of rug he had found on the walk and put it down for her.

"Oh my God," Crystal said.

"It's okay," Uncle Percy said. I told Crystal to sit down and gave CeCe back to her. I lit up a cigarette. By that point, my beard had started to grow and there wasn't anything I could do. Later that night I had to take a dump off the bridge and use baby wipes to clean myself. In that moment, I was so far from the glamorous diva I had just been. I wondered then if I'd ever be a diva again.

We slept on the bridge for damn near three days. On the last morning, I got up and went to relieve myself. I saw a woman cleaning a dirty diaper.

"You got any diapers?" she asked. "I got a baby, and this one is three days old." She held it up to show me.

"Hang on," I said and grabbed a clean diaper from Crystal's bag. I handed the new diaper to the lady and she started to cry— and then she put it on her baby. My main concern was we were almost out of formula, so Adam and I decided to go look for food and diapers. I told Crystal and Uncle Percy to stay in one spot, and me and Adam went in opposite directions. I spotted an Exxon station and we went to take cold drinks, chips, and, well, cigarettes. Nobody was buying anything in the city at that point, so call it looting, but it was survival. When I returned, Uncle Percy and Crystal and the baby were together. Adam wasn't back yet so we didn't move. One hour passed, two hours passed, and no Adam. We waited all damn night, but he never came back.

"What if something happened to Adam?" asked Crystal.

"He's gonna be fine," I said, and forced myself to believe it. That boy had spent enough time in jail to know how to survive anything. And the truth was, we couldn't wait anymore. People were starting to lose their composure.

"Where are these damn buses?" a man shouted to a National Guardsman. It was frustrating, all these guys standing around when women were using shit-filled diapers for their kids.

"They're coming, sir," this young kid answered, holding his gun on his right side. After a few more hours of waiting, we all decided that the buses weren't coming and the word in the camp was that the Superdome was full, so people were heading to the Convention Center.

I know most people saw the misery on the news that was the Superdome and the Convention Center, but, child, unless you were there, there's almost no way to picture it. People act stupid when they get scared. At the Convention Center, kids were raiding freezers of stores. They were taking out packs of frozen ribs and chicken breasts. "What you gonna do with that?" I asked a young boy in a white tank top, shorts, and no shoes.

"Fuck you," he said and kept walking.

The bathrooms were overflowing with so much shit and diarrhea that we were forced to sleep outside the Convention Center. We found a little spot and huddled close together. I lit up a cigarette not even knowing the brand.

"Hey, Big Freedia!" a woman barked as she walked by. I wanted to die. I had a full beard by then, for the first time in my life. I was anyone but the Queen Diva.

Lawd, when those buses finally came the next day, it was like a riot, fighting to get on them. Everyone wanted to get out. The National Guard had to hold us all back, so we wouldn't bum-rush the buses. Our turn finally came up and me and Uncle Percy stepped onto the bus. I turned around and there was Crystal, not moving.

"I ain't leaving Adam, ya heard me?" she said.

"Child, get on the bus!" I said, pulling her onto the stairs and pushing her and CeCe into the bus. She cried the whole ride. The airport was crowded but, baby, I was so relieved when we walked onto the plane. It was clean and there were seats for miles on that thing. I didn't even know where we were headed, but when you think you might die, anywhere is better than where you are.

The plane took us to an army base in Arkansas. The base had a church attached to it and oh my God, I will never forget the pastor. I can still see his white skin and long beard. He was an angel. He had clean beds waiting and gave us bags of new toiletries. I turned the shower water on extra hot and lathered my face with soap. I took a razor to my beard and shaved liked nobody's business.

The church people had made us all a fresh lunch. When I charged up my phone, the first thing I did was call my mom. She was hysterical.

"Momma, we all okay," I said. "But we lost Adam."

"Adam is okay, he called me!" she said between her tears. "He's in Arkansas." I yelled to Crystal that Adam was okay. "Get a bus ticket and come to Shreveport!" my momma said.

"Yes, Momma, I'll do it." The problem was I didn't have any cash and Crystal had spent her two hundred dollars. But I had the check for eight hundred from the insurance agency that came the day of the storm, so I asked the pastor if he could deposit it and give me the cash. He agreed and I bought us tickets to Shreveport for the following day.

At dinner, I felt a sense of relief I had not felt in days. I held

CeCe against my hip and hummed "Make Me a Blessing." She looked into my eyes and smiled. Singing was comforting in that moment, just like it had been all those years in church. I put her on the floor of the church and she pulled herself up on a bench, got steady on her little feet, and took her first steps.

CHAPTER 22
SPREADING THE GOSPEL

I N SEPTEMBER 2005, after arriving at the Shreveport bus stop, Ms V took us straight to LaPlace, a small town about forty minutes north of New Orleans. Reuniting with my momma after our harrowing experience will be etched in my memory forever. "My babies!" she hollered as we stepped off the bus. Keith was behind her. We huddled together at the bus depot—even Keith. Crystal sobbed and my mom cried and CeCe just smiled. I finally lost it too. I had held myself together all those days after the storm for the family, but I couldn't anymore.

All the poverty and tragedy of New Orleans life didn't prepare me for the effects of Katrina. Until you go through something like that, there's just no way to comprehend it, but it was like our lives got wiped out. I didn't know if I'd ever get my stuff from the apartment or if the building was even still standing. I had no clue if friends and extended family were alive or where they were. No one was allowed back in the city, so at that point, my mom and her refuge were all we had.

Ms. V and her family owned property in LaPlace. It's actually where my entire family on my mom's side is from, and my grandparents had left them a house. It was a little green-and-white five-bedroom house in need of repairs, but it had a roof. It had been vacant for decades, and the pipes and walls had cracks in them nine feet long. My mom and her sisters decided to take the opportunity to fix it up. As long as they could get on without bickering, which turned out to only be a few months, it was a place to rebuild.

This queen is no country boy, and there was zero nightlife in LaPlace. No clubs meant no way for me to earn a living, and that made me crazy. But I'm never one to stew too long in the negative. I knew I was gonna pick myself up and dust myself off—and I was gonna go back to New Orleans. But in the meantime, I needed to make a living. Katey said she had been picking up shows in Dallas. Kim had gone to Fort Worth, and she said there was Bounce in the clubs there. I had heard that DJs from home, like DJ Poppa and Silver, had already established residencies at some clubs in and around Texas. Because there were so many New Orleans transplants in these cities, the demand for Bounce was real.

Between my mom and Percy fighting over whether to put in new carpet or replace the stove, I was itching to get out. I had found out Hockey was in Atlanta with his family. I eventually got in contact with all my friends who had spread out around the South, but Texas was where the music was. One Monday when I was at the hardware store, picking up some paint for my mom, I got a call from a club promoter.

"This is Horse Man," he said. "I run things here in Houston."

"Okay," I said.

"The people here keep asking for Big Freedia, so I need to see what the fuck this guy is all about," he said. "You wanna come down here and play a gig?"

"Just tell me when and where," I told him.

"Breakers this Friday night," he said.

"See you there." My cousin Alison had relocated to Houston, so I called her and she said I could crash at her place. That next Thursday, I hauled my ass six hours to Houston in a rental car.

Breakers was a dive bar in the southwest part of the city. When I got there at about 11:30 p.m., the place was buzzing, and the smell of liquor and fresh weed immediately put me at ease.

"You Big Freedia?" a handsome young black man with a goatee and baseball cap asked.

"That's me," I said.

"Horse Man," he said, holding out his hand. As we shook hands, I took notice of his heavy gold chain and large diamond earrings.

"You got my money?" I said.

"Can you wait until after to settle?" Horse Man asked.

"Oh, no," I said, shaking my head, thinking of KT's sage advice.

"Right, right, I gotcha," he said, reaching in his pocket. "I respect that, Freedia," he added, handing me a thick wad of twenties.

By the time I hopped onstage, the place was almost filled all the way back to the bar. I started by riffing over some Bounce tracks and Mariah Carey's "You Will Always Be My Baby." But when I went into my own track, "Gin in My System," people started jumping up and down and hollering. The craziest thing is that people knew the lyrics.

While I was onstage, a woman walked up to the front and reached her hand up. "We need you here in Houston, Big Freedia," she said, and then her eyes teared up. I reached for her hand and held it.

"I'm here, honey," I said. "I'm not going anywhere." Watching her, I could feel her pain.

When I went backstage to thank Horse Man, he was counting dollar bills. "You be here next Friday?" he asked.

"Hell yes!" I said. For the next few months, I went back and forth between Houston and LaPlace every single week. Horse Man ran all the Houston spots, so he started to book me at Players Club, Breakers, and Breakers 2 on the weekends.

Over six months, I had developed a pretty good following in Texas, so between me and Katey, Sissy Bounce was steadily infiltrating the state.

There was so much raw emotion and grief that we were all holding on to, the shows were filled with unbridled energy. They started to become something more than simply a release from life's daily stresses. They were our salvation.

One weekend, Horse Man had booked a show at Players Club. "I'll get you a hotel so you can stay the weekend," he said. I called my friend and Bounce artist HaSizzle about getting some smoke for my trip since weed was the antidote for the long stretches of highway between LaPlace and Houston.

"Where my smoke at?" I asked.

"Hang on a minute," HaSizzle said, and I heard a ruffling on the phone.

"Hello," a young but gruff voice sounded on the other end. Something about his voice was sexy.

"Who is this?" I asked.

"Devon," he said.

"What's good, Devon?" I asked.

"Chillin'," he uttered, and laughed nervously. "You Big Freedia?

"Yes," I said.

"I've heard about you," he said. HaSizzle asked for the phone back.

"Take my number," I tried to say before Devon passed the phone back to HaSizzle.

"I'll be ready for you tomorrow morning," HaSizzle said before I could ask about his friend. Sure enough, that night Devon called and we talked for hours. He told me he stayed with his mom in St. Rose after the storm. He had seen some shows. *Fuck it*, I thought, *what did I have to lose?* "Wanna come with me to Houston tomorrow?" I asked. Those drives were long and lonely, so to me, I was just happy to have the company.

"Sure," he said.

"I'll scoop you up tomorrow once I get my stuff together," I said, feeling a surge of excitement. As I hung up the phone, I thought about Hockey. We hadn't broken up officially, but we just weren't clicking. He was seeing girls on the side or as a cover and I hated sharing him. It was expected that I would be okay that he was with girls, but I, on the other hand, was supposed to be loyal to him. Plus, we hadn't had sex in months and he refused to bring around his family and friends.

The next morning I soaked in the bath for a few extra minutes. I ripped open a new package of fresh white wifebeaters and laced up my Timbs, so excited I almost forgot my bag. I hopped in my new blue Chevy Avalanche that my mom signed for, and took off to meet my travel companion.

I called Devon to let him know I was outside. Out walked the finest boy you've ever seen, with a small book sack over his shoulder. "Oh yes," I murmured.

"Hi," he mumbled, throwing his bag into the backseat of the truck cab. I was arrested for a moment by his light brown eyes and his big juicy lips.

"What's good?" I asked, wiping the beads of sweat that started to appear on my head. When he plopped in the passenger seat, all I could see were his eyelashes, which went on forever.

"Not much," he said. Before departing, he rolled two blunts and we went off on our journey.

"How old are you?" I asked.

"Twenty-one," he said.

"You lying," I said, half joking.

"Okay, nineteen," he said. We talked the entire ride to Houston. Devon's grandmother had just died and it had hit him hard. He lived with his mother and siblings. There was something hard about him, but sweet too. I liked this kid.

As soon as we arrived in Houston, we checked into the hotel. Secretly pleased to see only one king-size bed, I quickly changed into my white jean vest, blue jeans, and my new red-and-white

Nike Dunks. I brushed the blue-streaked bangs off my face and put in some teardrop earrings, and I was ready.

When we got to the Players Club, the place was already near capacity. As we made our way through the crowd, the sweat from clubgoers made the place feel like a steam room. A rider of vodka, Hennessy, and Red Bull awaited us backstage.

"Help yourself," I told Devon and took out some Keep Moving cigars and started rolling a blunt.

The crowd was amped that night. I performed a freestyle I had become well known for, "Gin in My System." After my set, I went backstage and stuffed the remaining Hennessys and Red Bulls into my purse.

"Let's go," I said to Devon. I was ready to be back in that hotel room, alone with this boy. When we got to the room, I went to the bed and started to roll another blunt. Devon poured the Hennessy in a glass.

"You want some?" he asked, holding up the bottle.

"Nah," I said, firing up a blunt. As I puffed, he unbuttoned his shirt and let it fall to the floor. I got a look at his six-pack as he strode over to the bed and sat down beside me. All subtlety was lost when I reached for my purse and searched for a condom.

"You are cute, you know that, Devon?" I said. When he smiled back at me and flashed his shiny white teeth, it was all I could do not to grab his face and stick my tongue in his mouth.

"You are too," he mumbled, reaching for me. He started to unzip my pants, but only finished partway and then almost frantically started to undo his. I pulled down my pants and watched as he strapped on the condom, all the while not taking my eyes off his full, wet lips. When we were both naked, he turned me over and went inside. Hockey flashed through my head only for one second, but the moans of our pleasure sounded well into the night.

I didn't want to leave him, but the next day I had to take Devon back to St. Rose. When we pulled up in front of his momma's house, he stepped out of the car and walked around to my side. "Bye, Freedia," he said, leaning in and kissing me on the lips.

A couple of weeks later, Devon came to Houston with me again. Horse Man booked a show at Breakers. My shows in Houston became places of healing and transformation. It was like all Katrina refugees were coming for healing those Friday and Saturday nights. It was our church.

Devon did something that helped me figure something out about Hockey. After the show, we made our way to the bar. I ordered two vodka and pineapples. As we waited, Devon leaned over and locked lips with me. Right there, in front of the whole club. It was the first time I had a public display of affection with a guy. As a gay man being told not to flaunt my sexuality my whole life, it was such a relief to just be free to be who I was. After that night, I was hooked.

CHAPTER 23
HOME

ONE NIGHT IN EARLY 2007, my friend Chetta Jackson called me and said there were some openings in the Copper Creek apartments on Crowder Boulevard in New Orleans, and gave me a number to call. In less than a week, I had the keys to a brand-new apartment. I traveled to my mom's, got everything that was left of my belongings, and moved. I had a few pieces of furniture, but the small two-bedroom was mine and I was thrilled to be home.

Caesar's was the first club to reopen after Katrina. They started this night called FEMA Fridays. It was packed with Katrina victims every week. People had money then from their FEMA checks and they really came out. Other clubs started opening up again. I immediately started playing gigs.

Katrina had decimated the Ninth Ward—and just about the whole Sissy Bounce scene too. Chev and Vockah were gone, Katey stayed in Dallas doing her thing, so it was me and Nobby. After Katrina, me and Nobby killed it.

By that point, I was falling in love with Devon, whether or not I was willing to admit it. Hockey would call occasionally, mostly when he needed something. That said, we also hadn't officially broken up.

I could only carry on that charade for so long, though. One evening, I was cooking dinner for Devon when Hockey just showed up at my front door.

"Can I get some gas money?" Hockey asked. Devon popped his head out behind me. I introduced them. After some polite chatter, I handed Hockey a few bucks, and he left.

But it got real sticky after that. I told Devon that Hockey was just a friend. When Hockey asked about Devon, "he's my cousin" flew out of my mouth. I wasn't proud about lying, but I just wasn't ready to tell him that I had found someone else.

Over the next few months, I continued to spend time with both of them. Hockey didn't have a clue about Devon, but Devon was starting to get irritated about this kid coming around asking favors from me.

"Who is that guy?" Devon asked once after Hockey called me and asked to borrow a hundred dollars to fix his car.

"Just an old friend," I lied. It came to a head one night when me, Hockey, Adam, and this girl Adam was dating, Stelita, were over at my place having dinner. I'm not gonna lie, Stelita was messy—and that bitch ran her mouth. We were all gathered in Ms. V's backyard smoking when out of nowhere, Stelita started in.

"I can't stand Freedia's new boyfriend," she said.

Hockey shot me a glare. "Freedia's new boyfriend?" he said narrowing his eyes. I was too scared to respond.

"Yeah: Devon," Stelita said, shooting me a smirk.

"You told me that was your cousin!" Hockey said, coughing from the blunt.

"I know," I said. "I didn't know how to tell you."

"Come on, girl," Adam said, grabbing Stelita's arm and leading her into the house.

Under the starlit sky, I took a puff of smoke. I felt relieved in a way. Maybe Stelita did me a favor.

"Why'd you lie?" Hockey asked.

I felt disgusted with myself. "I'm sorry, Hockey. I've really wanted to tell you."

"Bitch, I'm so mad at you, I could kill you," he said.

"What about you and your girlfriend?"

Hockey stood up. "You know my situation."

"I'm tired of it," I said. "I can't do it anymore, Hockey."

"I'm gonna go, Freddie," he said. I crushed my cigarette into the ground and walked him to the door. He put out his hand and I grabbed it. I held it for a moment and then let go.

When I shut the door and turned around, Adam and Stelita were on the couch watching TV.

"Messy-ass ho!" I said, grabbing my purse and walking out the door.

CHAPTER 24
THE CROSSOVER

ON AUGUST 12, 2008, *Gambit Weekly*, a New Orleans alternative paper, published an article called "Sissy Strut," which ruffled a lot of feathers in the Bounce community. Alison Fensterstock, the *Gambit*'s music columnist at the time, wrote the story. It's important to make it clear here that Alison was one of the very first white girls to get hip to me and the other sissies. And she was by all accounts the first journalist to document the scene in a major media outlet, so I got nothing but love for her.

It was the headline, "Sissy Strut," that people latched on to, and when they did, it took on a life of its own. Other media outlets ran with it and Sissy Bounce became a label that stuck. For me and some other sissies, the distinction felt like we were being sidelined. We had worked so hard to be taken as seriously as Mannie Fresh and Master P, and now with one article, we were something different.

Since then, I really don't feel strongly about it one way or another. Fact is, we are different from the straight Bounce artists. Our music is more sexually explicit and, frankly, more fun! As long as I'm making music, I'm happy.

BY 2009, ME AND NOBBY were running the club scene together. I was starting to feel like I had hit a plateau and that there was something more, something bigger that I wanted to do, but I wasn't sure what it was.

Then I met Rusty Lazer. Now, if you're from New Orleans, second-line bands are part of life, so I'm going to explain it here once: Every Sunday we have a street parade. The main line is the band at the front leading, usually a brass band. The second line are the group of folks who follow the parade, toasting, dancing. Nearly every neighborhood in New Orleans has these parades every month or so. These second-line clubs get intricate and there are queens of the different parades.

The second-line club called VIP Ladies asked me to be their queen for a day; the festivities included a parade. I bought a crisp pair of white pants and a matching suit jacket. I also bought a rust-colored shirt with a white collar and I searched all over town for a pair of matching red shoes. My hair was spiked up and two silver stripes went all the way to the top. Since I was queen, I sat in the back of a convertible and threw beads and waved to people as we rode through the streets. Midway through the parade, we stopped for a break. As I leaned back in the convertible, downing my second bottle of water, a skinny little white guy with the craziest handlebar mustache approached me. He introduced himself as Rusty Lazer.

"I'm a DJ," he continued. "I've been playing your music for people all over the world—and they love it!"

"Really?" I said, trying to wrap my head around the fact that there's this seemingly straight dude who says his friends all over the world love my music. I was skeptical, but definitely curious.

"Yes," he said. "I've deejayed all over the world—Berlin, China, and Japan—and play your music. People love you!"

"Really?" I said, only half believing him.

"Can I come to one of your shows?" he asked.

"Of course," I said, appreciating his enthusiasm. "Come to Caesar's tomorrow."

Rusty showed up that following night, and for about a good six months kept coming to my shows. It was always easy to spot him since he was usually the only white speck in a club of black folks. We kept talking and I started to trust Rusty. The thing that I came to learn about him was that he was a true music lover. He had been in some kind of new wave folk band before Katrina and was passionate about the city and culture of New Orleans. He was also part of this queer-friendly punk scene that I didn't even know existed. I always thought punk rock was that really aggro music by skinheads. Apparently a new, postpunk scene was developing, and Rusty was part of it.

In January 2009, Rusty said he wanted to put together a "Sissy

Bounce Sweethearts Ball" for Valentine's Day with me, Katey Red, and Sissy Nobby at One Eyed Jacks. I was confused for a couple reasons. First, One Eyed Jacks was a very well-established music venue in the French Quarter, for white people. Second, at that point Rusty was known in some circles as a musician, but he didn't have juice as a promoter.

When I questioned him on both, he said, "Freedia, we can expand this movement." He enlisted the help of the writer Alison Fensterstock from *Gambit Weekly* and her husband, Lefty Parker, who ran the Circle Bar. Turned out they were instrumental in convincing the promoters at One Eyed Jacks that sissy rappers could fill their club.

"I love it," I said. Katey and Nobby were in too.

We promoted the night all month long. We covered all the clubs with flyers and these cool fancy posters we made. Also, by that point I was bringing this dancer Raquel Singelton from the Sixth Ward, aka Rocky, with me to all my local punk shows. She had been a loyal dancer and proved herself to be reliable.

As I picked out my outfit the night of the show, my stomach was in a knot. I kept it simple: black jeans and a white T-shirt, a vest with my Chicago Cubs baseball cap and my new hoop earrings I had scored at the mall.

Once I got to the club, I saw Nobby.

"Guuuurrllll," she huffed, "I don't know about this."

"God got us, bitch, don't worry," I said, feeling the sweat on my palms. As we made our way through the crowd, I could feel the sweat on my forehead. It was a sea of like four hundred white people. Nobby stopped and looked back at me, her eyes widening. "Go!" I said, pushing her toward the back of the club.

The proper backstage and our rider of food and drinks temporarily distracted me from my nerves. There were couches, dressing rooms, and refreshments! Katey was already there, in a dazzling red dress and magnificent flowing hair down her back.

"Bitch, we gonna perform 'Big Freddie Kay Ready'?" Katey asked me.

"Yeah," I said. "Let's come out at the end and perform that together."

I watched Katey walk around backstage, primping herself: She didn't appear nervous at all. I always admired that about her.

Rusty called me and Nobby just then. It was our time. We walked out onto the stage with Rocky following closely behind. I started with "Azz Everywhere," and Nobby shook her behind. Then, as I was performing "Gin in My System," I remember looking out into the crowd and seeing so many asses shaking! This young girl in a pink baby-doll dress was singing the lyrics. The crowd was going wild! When Katey and I did our encore the crowd started screaming and jumping up and down. People got out their video cameras, their phones. It was amazing.

After the show, I walked out into the crowd. I spotted Rusty at the bar.

"Great show!" he said. I was high from excitement. "I want you to check out my friend," he said, pointing to this white girl on the dance floor. "Her name is Altercation."

This girl was comin' for answers: She wore fishnet stockings, a bra top with a net shirt over it, and some booty shorts. Her ass was moving like a wave of water.

"She not playin'." I had never seen a white girl who had an ass that could clap.

"I think we should bring her on for your shows," Rusty said and walked away. I saw him go up to her and whisper something in her ear. I thought having both Altercation and Rocky would be a hot look. She walked over to me and introduced herself.

"I love you!" she said, her face speckled with glitter. There was something innocent and sweet about Altercation. She was strange to me, but I liked her.

"Thank you, baby, you sure can move!" I said. "You're giving me life! You might have to dance for me one day!"

"Of course!" she said, displaying her warm smile. From that point, Altercation became one of my main dancers. What I didn't learn until later is just how deep into the culture of Bounce she was. Altercation was already teaching classes on the history of dance around New Orleans. She knew the roots of twerking and how it was passed down from our ancestors in West Africa. There's actually a dance called the Mapouka dance that involves the thrusting of the hips just like shaking. It was from her that I learned the origins myself. Altercation had done her homework.

She told me that she saw the dance one night in New Orleans, fell in love with it, and was completely self-taught. That bitch got balls to go into the black clubs like she did and just start to cut it up.

"Come out tomorrow to 2001," I said. Altercation nodded and

just then the girl I'd spotted in the baby-doll dress tapped my shoulder.

"Hi, Big Freedia!" she gushed. "I love your music!" I just couldn't believe that any of these people knew me. That was a real turning point for me: I could bring this Bounce thing to the next level—the national level.

That summer, Rusty had another idea: to go to New York and do a minitour with me and Sissy Nobby. He said he had a jewelry designer friend, Arielle De Pinto, who wanted us to perform at her trunk show near Soho and that he'd try to book some more shows to make it worth the trip.

"Of course," I said. I had never been to New York before.

"I know someone who can put us up in Brooklyn," he said. I was starting to realize that Rusty really did know people in every city. He was like a punk rock Gypsy.

As it turned out, Rusty was able to book five other shows, one of which was at Glasslands in Williamsburg, Brooklyn, with the artist Spank Rock. The others were Happy Ending and at the Chicken Hut in Brooklyn, which was a punk party. I had never heard of any of them but I was excited to see New York!

Nobby's manager had booked her ticket separately, so she was landing a few hours before me, Rusty, and Altercation. When we landed, I got a text from Nobby: "I don't like this place." I texted her to wait until we go there, hoping she wasn't gonna start fussin' before one show. Something can set that bitch off and there's no bringing her back.

When we pulled up in the cab to the house, I knocked on the

door. A tall man of Middle Eastern descent opened the door but didn't let us in. He had a very intense stare on his face. Nobby walked up behind him.

"You can't stay here," he barked at us.

"What?" I asked. "What happened?"

"Your friend," he said and pointed to Nobby. "He didn't say a word to me. He is so rude." Nobby was doing the neck roll.

"Get out! All of you!" the man said. We backed away down the stairs and onto the sidewalk.

"Girl, what the fuck are you doing?" I said to Nobby. "Why didn't you speak to that man?" I was heated.

"Hell no, bitch," she said, waving her finger at me and flipping her phone open. "Get me home!" she yelled into the phone.

"We got five shows!" I said. "You ain't leaving."

"Oh, yes, I am!" she said, still on the phone. She huffed and walked off, leaving me, Rusty, and Altercation right there on the sidewalk.

I fired up a cigarette.

"We gonna do this?" Rusty looked at me. "I can get us somewhere else to stay."

"What am I supposed to do?" I said. "We were both supposed to perform."

"You're gonna do it solo," he said.

I contemplated for a minute. "Let's do it."

Rusty found another friend for him and Altercation to stay with, and somehow convinced Arielle de Pinto to let me stay with her. That night we played at the jewelry opening for Arielle. It was in a warehouse in Soho. There must have been close to two hundred people. The scene was something I had never seen before: lots of rail-thin white girls sporting outlandish but fashionable clothes. There was a flamboyant man with thigh-high boots and a furry hat spinning and sashaying around the room all night.

"This is the downtown art scene," Rusty said. He must have seen my wide-eyed reaction to it all. I had never performed for a crowd like that. What are all these rich art people going to think of me?

Arielle walked over and handed me a microphone. There was no stage, just a slightly raised platform for me. I started with "Y'all Get Back Now" and the crowd was moving. Then "Gin in My System." People were very excited and into it. I couldn't believe this small crowd was getting so into this music.

The next morning I was even more excited when Rusty called to tell me that he'd heard from the marketing director at American Apparel, Marsha Brady. She was at the show and loved us so much, she invited us to come by the store that day.

"Let's go!" I said. I told Rusty and Altercation to meet me at the hotel. From there we hopped the subway to the American Apparel at Broadway and Great Jones Street. We walked in and asked for Marsha. She walked out and greeted us. You could tell she was important. She led us around the store. "Take what you want," she said, pointing to clothes on the racks. I had never heard such a proposition.

"*Anything?*" I asked, looking at Rusty and Altercation in disbelief.

"Anything," Marsha said, smiling. I spotted a white T-shirt with the words "Legalize Gay" across it. I took one. Holding it up, I said, "Thank you, Marsha."

"Come on. I said take what you want." She handed me, Rusty, and Altercation each a plastic shopping bag.

"What size are you?" Marsha asked me.

"Large," I said. She grabbed like three sweatshirts and four shirts off the racks and handed them to me. I put them in my bag. I spotted a pair of red underwear that had "Legalize Gay" sprawled across the ass and slowly placed them into the bag. Soon enough, I just went for it: I took a shiny gold jacket and a black Liquid jacket. As I jammed a red jacket in the bag, I looked up at Rusty, who was trying on some glasses. I grabbed socks, shorts, and leggings. I felt this rush, like this is what it's like to be a rock star and get free things. Also, to be poor your whole life and then be able to walk into a store and take whatever you want? It was like a dream.

Altercation, Rusty, and I walked down Broadway that day with full bags. I felt high. I could get used to this, I thought.

That night we had the Glasslands show with this kid Naeem who went by Spank Rock. He is an alternative punk techno artist from Philly. I had never heard of him at the time, but apparently he was a big deal because the place was packed. I walked in with my new shirt, my thick gold necklace, and my long, dangling earrings. The butterflies in my stomach were in full effect. We went back-stage and met Naeem, a small, skinny black dude with thick glasses.

"Hey, Freedia!" he said, opening his arms for a hug. "Thanks so much for coming out."

"Sure," I said, embarrassed that I didn't know who he was.

"I'm so happy to finally meet you," he said. His warm welcome helped quell the butterflies.

When it was time for me to get onstage, Naeem did something that I will never forget and am very grateful for to this day. Not only did he play before me, which was quite an honor, but he quieted the crowd after his set.

"I know you all are here for Spank Rock," he announced over the mic, "but we have someone really special here tonight. Her name is Big Freedia and when you see this show tonight, you are going to lose your mind!" Rusty was in place at the DJ booth. Altercation and me walked on, and I started with "Azz Everywhere." Everyone in the crowd started screaming. Then all of a sudden girls bent over and started shakin' their asses. I pulled a girl with a pierced lip and tattoos all up her leg up onto the stage and she went hard. Next I performed "Gin in My System." I remember looking out into the crowd and being shocked: they were singing the lyrics!

The shows at Chicken Hut and Happy Ending were more of the same, except bigger and rowdier crowds.

The day after the Chicken Hut show, a writer from the magazine *Fader* called Rusty and requested an interview with me. At that point I had been covered in the New Orleans press, but not any national press. I was nervous, but didn't let on.

The next day, we went to the offices on the ninth floor of a building on Twenty-third Street in Manhattan. They sat me in a chair and a kid with a camera walked over to me.

"This gonna be on camera?" I asked. I hadn't put any makeup on or anything.

"Yes, it's for Fader TV," the kid said. "It's our Internet station."

"Okay," I said, trying to play it off. They turned the camera on and started to shoot questions at me. The interview was supposed to take thirty minutes but it took about an hour. This girl had so many questions about my life and I needed my cigarette breaks.

When we finally finished, I asked, "Where can people see this?"

"Everywhere," he said. "All over America. All over the world."

"The world?" I repeated.

"Yes, London, Australia, Stockholm?"

"Oh my Gawd," I said, smiling. Who knew? I could feel I had just taken a big step forward. It was a good feeling.

When we finally got on the plane to go home, I was exhausted. But two very important things came out of that trip, besides the exposure. We had a press package and enough footage of shows to make an electronic press kit, a critical tool an artist needs to book shows and build a name.

"How about we do a Big Freedia greatest hits album?" Rusty asked as the plane was taking off.

"Greatest hits?" I said. "Baby, I'm not Jay Z. I don't even have a real, national album out yet."

"Exactly," said Rusty. "That's why I think we should do it."

THE MINUTE WE GOT BACK to New Orleans, friends were blowing up my phone claiming Nobby was running her mouth saying she had a family emergency and that's why she had to leave New York. Typical Nobby: clicks out for no reason and then can't even own up to it. Lawd, I was trying to be patient with her, because we made a great team on stage and I knew Nobby didn't have a family. Being all alone in the world had to be hard, but her behavior jeopardized her friendships—and her career.

It wasn't long after Brooklyn that Rusty started booking shows out of town. The gigs paid very little but I knew getting in front of this new audience was going to pay off for me. Rusty was getting me national exposure.

Just as we were making moves, my momma gave me some terrible news. I was on tour with Rusty, Altercation, and Rocky. We were in Kansas City when she called. She had seen her doctor, Dr. Evans, and needed me, Crystal, and Adam to come to the house together. That wasn't good. In my whole life, my mom never asked to see all three of her children at once.

In addition to my momma, Devon was blowing up my phone that night. They always say tour life is bad for relationships and it had put a strain on ours for sure. Devon would get aggravated when he couldn't reach me. This would become an irritating, and constant, issue between us.

I didn't say anything to my dancers or Rusty that night. I just rolled a blunt and tried to shut my mom and Devon out of my mind. But something powerful happened in Kansas. The lights blinded me as I walked onstage with my mic in one hand and a towel in the other. I looked back at Rusty and heard the first beats to "Gin in My System."

"I've got that gin in my system," I sang, and the audience responded, "Somebody gonna be my victim!" The club was packed. A girl with pink hair and a pierced eyebrow climbed up on a rafter of the stage and started twerking. "I love you, Freedia!" she kept shouting. In that moment, a sense of calm washed over me. That was the point when I realized the audience was my congregation now. I rapped for money and because I loved it. But right then, it truly was my salvation. I'd been through so much. As I watched Altercation and Rocky—and the audience members I brought up onstage—wiggle, bounce, and shake, I realized it was healing us all.

I got home from tour the next day and went straight to my mom's house. My whole family was there. When she told us she had spinal and lung cancer, my hands started shaking and I broke out into a sweat, but I wasn't gonna let her see.

"They're giving me a few months," she said. Crystal started to sob. Adam stared at the floor.

"We're gonna get through this, Mom," I said, trying to sound confident. "God got you."

CHAPTER 25

INTERGALACTIC EXPERIENCE

AS IT TURNED OUT, New York brought about lots of good things. Too bad for Nobby. She missed out on everything. The first thing was that the car company Scion had agreed to release a five-song EP, which was titled *Scion A/V Presents: Big Freedia*.

The second thing to come out of that trip was I got a booking agent. In March 2010, Bojan Jovanovic, from the Windish Agency in Chicago, reached out to Rusty and asked for some footage of my show. A punk rock promoter named Sean Carlson had been to one of the New York shows and apparently he called Bojan. Not only is Windish one of the top booking agencies in the country, but I heard that Bojan was their highest-earning agent, second only to the boss, Tom Windish. Bojan was booking all the sickest electro-punk bands at the time—Designer Drugs, Best Coast, and SSION. Within hours of us sending him footage of our shows and the *Fader* video, Bojan called and offered me a 10 percent deal, with no exclusivity, which meant he took 10 percent off the top, and I could book with other agents as well. Considering I had never had a real booking agent, I jumped at the chance to sign.

Within weeks, Windish booked me for a tour with Galactic, an epic funk band from New Orleans who were signed to Sony. I knew Ben Ellman, the group's producer and saxophonist. He had always been down for Bounce. In spite of being in one of the biggest bands in America, he was always trying to link up with underground rappers and give them shine.

Sometime in 2009, Ben rang me up and asked me to record a song with them for a new joint they were working on, *Ya-Ka-May*. Ben had corralled all the hot New Orleans acts, Nobby, Katey Red, Cheeky Blakk, and Mystikal. I will never forget the Galactic studios on the corner of Amelia and Tchoupitoulas streets. I'm talking a mixing board the size of a room, a Moog synthesizer, and the best microphones money could buy.

When I arrived I was so relieved to find only Ben and an engineer in the place, laying down some experimental tracks. To put me at ease with recording, Ben played a Triggerman beat. "I'll lay your part over our instrumentation, once we've got the recording," he said. When I heard the beat, inspiration just came to me:

Double it, double it, double it, double it, double it
Double it, double it, double it, double it, double it
Double it, double it, double it, double it, double it.

I'm Freedia, I'm so Josephina
Josephine, if you know what I meana.

Ben knew exactly what I meant. "You killed it!" he said right into my earphones. "I guess it's called 'Double It.'"

I'm not the type of emcee who is known for my elaborate lyrics. That's not Bounce. The way it works with me is that I feel a beat and then chant or riff. It's all about the rhyming, the rhythm, and the repetition. And, since for sissies it's all about what neighborhood you rep, I added Josephina, my own twist on Josephine Street.

Working with Ben was a blast, so when the band asked me to open for them a year later, I was like, Hell mothafucking yes! The tour was only three dates, at five bills for each show, but I wasn't doing it for the money. The Galactic audience was a whole new booty-shaking fan base. I was excited: We were booking it to San Francisco, the gay mecca, and a city I had dreamed of visiting my whole life. And not just San Francisco! We were doing the Fillmore theater—world class!

Me and Rusty shared one room and the dancers—Altercation and Rocky—shared another room at some raggedy hotel in the Tenderloin district. Being from the hood myself, you'd think nothing would faze me, but the masses of homeless and junkies all up and down the streets of San Francisco shocked me.

When I heard that the Fillmore held four thousand people and the show was sold out, I thought I was going to throw up so much that I'd never leave the hotel bathroom. The fact that my purple checked jacket was very wrinkled when I took it out of my bag didn't help matters.

"Freedia!" Rocky was pounding the door as I tried to smooth out the jacket with steam from a hot shower.

"What you want?" I said, opening the door.

"Want some?" She was holding a huge bag of McDonald's.

"No, baby, I'm too nervous to think about food," I said, and returned to the bathroom to dab some new sparkly silver liner to my eyelids. My mom called just then.

"Momma, I'm nervous," I said.

"Baby, they are gonna love you," she reassured me.

Just then, Rusty was yelling for us to go.

"Gotta run, Mom, love you," I said. I told Rusty I'd meet them all in front of the hotel. I hurried down the stairs to the street to smoke a blunt before we had to get into the cab.

The Fillmore was amazing. We dashed through the back door, where a kid with a Motörhead T-shirt and a walkie-talkie checked our credentials. The backstage was huge. We even had our own dressing room with our name scratched out with pen directly next to Galactic's name.

I learned quickly that performing on a stage of that size is totally different than the tiny ones we were used to. I hadn't anticipated the fact that two dancers can look insignificant on a big stage. "Girls, move around on that stage, ya heard me?" I told Rocky and Altercation before we went on. Rusty had his computer queued up with "Diva Is a Female Hustler."

As any opening act knows, no one wants to be the one to get out onstage and work a crowd that is waiting for another band. Luckily, if there was one thing I'd learned in my years at the clubs, it was how to get a crowd hyped!

Rusty went on first. He started to warm up the crowd with Beyoncé's "Diva": "Na, na, na, diva is a female version of a hustler." Then I sent Rocky and Altercation out. When I walked on, the lights blinded me, which might have been a good thing. I couldn't see the fact that there were only a few people milling about.

After "Diva," the "Azz Everywhere" beat came on. The tiny crowd was completely still. The dancers started to cut it up. What I noticed was that when Altercation danced, people started to move. It became very clear then just how much she could help with crossing over to the white audience. It was like once they saw a white girl clapping her ass, bending over, twerking, and shaking, they realized that it wasn't just something black women could do. As we did "Gin in My System" and by "Rock Around the Clock" people started to flock to the front of the stage.

Rusty was hustling. He booked house parties, gigs, after-parties—whatever he could to bring in some extra dough—before and after each show. So as soon as we were done with the Galactic show, me, Rusty, and the dancers packed all our gear and bags and cabbed it to Studs, a gay bar south of Market Street. We did a short set to the mostly male audience and it went off. People didn't know what they were seeing, but they were screaming and waving their hands and jumping up and down. When we finished at Studs, we jammed over to a house party in Oakland.

"I need a burger. Is there a Five Guys around here?" Rocky said as the cab made its way through the streets of San Francisco to the Bay Bridge.

"You all hungry again?" I asked. They had eaten at the hotel.

"I want sushi," Altercation said.

"I don't do fish," Rocky said. That was a constant battle on the road. Rusty and Altercation usually wanted some kind of healthy food, while Rocky and I wanted greasy food that felt like home.

I spied a Jack in the Box drive-thru on the side just before the on-ramp to the bridge. I knew Altercation and Rusty weren't gonna love it, but we needed food and really didn't have time to look or sit down somewhere.

"Stop here!" I told the driver. Rocky and Altercation ordered a whole burger and fries apiece and finished them off before we made it to Oakland.

It may sound cliché, but we really did become a family on the road. I felt like—and I still feel like—every one of my dancers is my child. My kids can be wild, especially the girls, with their specific needs, tantrums, and attitude, ya heard me? But I love each and every one of them.

THE NEXT DAY we hopped a flight to Los Angeles, another city I was dying to see. I remember flying over palm trees and pools at LAX for the first time. It was exactly as I pictured it. Billboards for *Sex and the City 2* lined the streets. I was in Hollywood!

Our gig was at the El Rey Theatre on Wilshire Boulevard with Galactic; it was another huge venue. After the show, Rusty booked us at a party at this small restaurant-bar in Silver Lake called El Cid. Wednesday nights belonged to the ultrahip party promoter duo who call themselves A Club Called Rhonda. We were going to do a short three-song set. El Cid was a typical cantina-type bar. It was tiny, could hold maybe two hundred people. The backstage was under a staircase and the size of a closet. The overpowering smell of cigarettes and tequila instantly comforted me.

El Cid was packed and filled with hipsters and gender benders. These are guys who wear dresses, girls who don't identify as gay or straight, and everything in between. I've come to realize that kids today look at sexuality on a continuum. I don't claim to speak for this group, but I think the fact that I'm feminine without being a drag queen or transsexual draws them to me.

We started with "Gin in My System" and from jump, people went wild! I would sing, "I want that gin in my system," and the crowd would answer, "Somebody's gonna be my victim!"

There were girls and boys just shaking. People went nuts when this very large girl jumped up onto the stage and started to shake her ass. I just started to pluck people from the audience. There must have been ten people twerking onstage. When we were done, the crowd started chanting, "Big Freedia! Big Freedia!" We ended up doing two more songs.

After the encore, I plopped down on a cooler backstage and lit up a cigarette. "You killed, honey," I said to Altercation.

"That was amazing!" she said. Rusty started packing his bag.

"You're sneaky, Rusty," Rocky suddenly shouted. She was mad and I had no idea why.

I looked at Rusty. He was good at defusing situations like this, but I wondered what she meant.

"What's up, Rocky?" I said.

"Rusty knows what I mean," she said, shaking her head. "He got his money, Freedia. Where is ours?" I wasn't sure if she was drunk or really saw something, but this wasn't the time to start shit.

"We'll get our money, honey," I said. Rusty always broke us off after the shows.

"I don't know what you're talking about," Rusty said and he walked out of the room. "I'll be right back, Freedia," he said. "Someone wants to meet you."

A couple minutes later, Rusty came back into the room with the most stunning Indian girl (I learned later that she was from Sri Lanka) I thought I'd ever seen. "I have someone I want you to meet," he said. "This is M.I.A."

My heart just about stopped. This was around the time the song "Paper Planes" was an international hit; she was major! I knew she was controversial, but I really didn't know what all that was about. I just knew she was an extraordinary performer.

"Hi," I said. I could not take my eyes off her.

"I loved the show," she said. "We need to do some music together."

"Yes, honey," I said, feeling like I might burst with excitement. Before I could say more, some guy whisked her away.

"Nice meeting you!" she said, and waved to me and Rusty.

"Bye, baby," I said and turned to Rusty. Before I could say anything, he said, "Dude! Lady Gaga saw the El Cid show. And she wants to work with you!"

"Oh my God" was all I could say. "Whaaaaaaat?"

"Yes, her manager told me and gave me his phone number! She's working on a new album and wants you to be on it!" I remember when we got back to the hotel that night I couldn't sleep one bit. I called my mom in the middle of the night and told her Lady Gaga saw me and wanted to work with me.

"I knew they'd love you," she said. "But, boy, it's four in the goddamn morning, now let me get some sleep!"

I woke up late the next day. Rusty was already packing. I called Rocky and Altercation and told them to get ready to head back to the airport.

Rocky was convinced that Rusty had skimmed money off the top that night and wouldn't let it go that day, but I was still so high from meeting M.I.A. and knowing Gaga wanted to work with me, I wasn't gonna let some inner-team fussing bother me. Looking back, this was a very special time in my career. It was like we were strapped to the front of a train that was speeding down the tracks. Things were just happening. There wasn't a calculated marketing or press plan like today.

Also at this point, Rusty was deejaying my shows, but the thing is, he was tour managing and pretty much managing me. The problem was, we never talked about it and we never had paperwork. This would come back to haunt us both, but at the time, it worked. He would get paid for deejaying and I'd pay him a percentage of the shows he booked. His fee varied, depending on what we made, who we had to pay, and our travel expenses.

A couple days after we returned to New Orleans, Rusty called me and said Windish had booked us at Fuck Yeah Fest, one of the biggest punk festivals in the country, to be held in Los Angeles in September.

"A punk festival?" I said into my phone.

"Yes, Freedia, it's perfect!" he said, always enthusiastic about these things.

"Don't punks hate gays?"

"No," Rusty explained. "This is a new breed. They're just misfits. It's about an attitude. You represent the punk rock attitude."

"Let's do it," I said.

AROUND 2010, me and Altercation started to hold Bounce classes together before shows, as a way to make extra cash. I liked the idea of putting the culture into context for people and Altercation was already teaching a Bounce class, so we just expanded on that.

Windish agreed to help us book the sessions, and they were very popular, especially in the college markets. Altercation would start by saying, "We're gonna get in touch with our inner pussies today," which would always get big laughs from the crowd. We'd go into the history and roots, and then we'd have hands-on twerking, bouncing, shaking, and wiggling lessons.

In July 2010, I was performing with Rusty at the Teen Summit, at the Pontchartrain Center in Kenner. We had just gotten to Kenner and I was puffing on a cigarette backstage when my phone beeped. It was Hockey's girlfriend, Tracy.

She was hysterical. "They shot him, they shot him," she just kept repeating.

"What?" I said. "What are you talking about?"

"Hockey is dead!" she managed to get out.

My head was spinning. "Where are you?" I asked.

"The house," she said.

"I'll be right there," I said. I told Rusty I had to go. I must have looked like hell because he didn't even ask why. I ducked out to the parking lot. When I got to Tracy's house, my adrenaline was pumping so hard, I almost forgot to put my car in park before getting out.

I walked up slowly to the scene. The cops were already there, the red and blue lights swirling. The house was taped off and neighbors were already gathering on the sidewalk. The first thing I saw was Hockey's car in the driveway, covered in bullet holes. When I spied his body on the street, memories flashed through my mind. Meeting him at the Middle Store, all the late-night talks, and cooking smothered chicken for him.

I tried to run to him, but a cop grabbed me and held me back. "It's a crime scene, sir," he said. "Are you a relative of the victim?"

I looked at him. "No."

"How do you know him?" he asked.

"He's my friend," I answered stoically.

"You have to stay behind the yellow line," the cop said.

Tracy came out, half-dressed, her face swollen from crying, black mascara running down her face. "He was shot twenty-five times," she said.

"Who the fuck did this?" I asked.

"I don't know," she said. "He was supposed to testify as an eyewitness in court tomorrow." I put my hands over my face and wept.

* * *

HOCKEY'S FUNERAL was at a church in the Ninth Ward, but I can't recall the name. It was all kind of a fog. I went numb as I prepared the lilies and carnations for the service.

Even more painful, I felt like a total stranger as I walked into the church that day. No one knew who I was, but I was Hockey's first love. His real love. A secret he had hidden all those years. As I searched the place for an empty seat, a woman in the front row turned around and stood up. As soon as our eyes met, I recognized Hockey's nose and eyes. It was his momma.

"Freddie?" she said, her eyes swollen.

I nodded instinctively, shocked that she did know who I was.

"Come here," she said, waving me over, the same hand grasping tissues.

I walked over tentatively, wondering how she knew me and what she knew of me.

"Sit here," she said, pointing to the seat next to her. I stepped past some people already seated and took the spot by Hockey's mom. We hugged but said nothing. There was nothing to say. I sang along to "Pass Me Not, O Gentle Savior" and "Amazing Grace," hoping the songs would bring me some peace. At the end of the service Hockey's mom turned to me and said, "He loved you, Freddie."

"Thank you," I said, trying to stay composed. When the service was over, I went to the repast. When it was time to leave, I got into my car, leaning my head back on the seat. As a flood of tears started streaming down my face, I thought, *This might be impossible to get over.*

CHAPTER 26
BOSS

Iᴛ ᴡᴀs ᴊᴜsᴛ ᴀғᴛᴇʀ ᴛʜᴀᴛ ᴛʀɪᴘ that Melvin "Mel" Foley, aka Boss Hogg, came into the picture. One night during FEMA Friday at Caesar's this hefty black man with dreadlocks and a diamond earring tapped my shoulder. He introduced himself to me as Boss and said he managed some of the biggest commercial Bounce artists, like Juvenile, B.G., Choppa, and Baby Boy.

"I've been watching you for a long time," he said. "I can do things for your career." We talked for a while. He told me that he had a company called Boss Hogg Entertainment with his "partna," Christopher Young, and they were interested in managing me and Nobby. Boss was cool. I was curious. "Give me a call if you're interested," he said, handing me his card.

Boss actually hit me up me a few times before I agreed to work with him. "Why don't you and Nobby come by the office, and I'll give you the contracts to look over. Chris can manage Nobby, and I'll manage you."

I called Nobby and she agreed to meet them. Of course, Nobby was very excited about being managed by Boss, because she didn't have someone like Rusty booking shows. The question was, could she even keep herself together long enough for a manager to help?

Boss's office was at his house on the West Bank, in Marrero. We walked through a charming garden of ficus trees to get to the front door. A cocker spaniel stayed right at my side as we walked into his living room. Boss led us past some black leather couches into a huge office. Gold plaques of Juvenile and Baby Boy adorned the walls. I envisioned one with my name on it.

"Look this over," he said, handing me and Nobby contracts. "And let me know what you guys think."

"Okay," I said, nodding my head.

"Yes, yes!" Nobby said, a bundle of nervous energy. Bitch was acting so eager, I thought she was gonna sign the paper right there without even reading it. Mel led us outside and we sat in some lawn chairs overlooking an inviting swimming pool.

"You got any questions?" Mel said.

"No," said Nobby.

"I do," I said. "If Rusty and I are booking our own shows, what will you do?"

"The way I see it," Boss said, resting his glass of soda on the table, "Rusty got the white crowd. I'll get the Chitlin' Circuit."

Made sense. I didn't want to abandon my fan base, who were mostly black women at that point. Rusty could get the cities like New York, Portland, and San Francisco, and Boss could focus on the South.

Of course, I had to think about how Rusty was going to feel if I signed a management contract with Mel. I knew Rusty had done a lot for me, but he really wasn't a manager. I didn't even think he wanted to be one. He was a musician. I felt someone like Mel, an experienced manager, could be exactly what I needed.

I called Rusty that day and told him that I was going to start Boss off with some tour managing, and Rusty seemed fine with it. I was about to go on another tour to B.O.M.B. Fest, a charity festival in Danbury, Connecticut, so the timing was perfect.

A few weeks later, Rusty called me. "Gaga's manager called today," he said. "Interscope doesn't think a Big Freedia guest feature is right for her."

"What does that even mean?" I barked.

"It means the label is scared to take a risk," Rusty said, "or something."

My heart felt like it was going to hit the floor.

"Can we call her directly?" I said. "Is there something we can do?"

"I don't think we should push it," Rusty said. "Things are incredible for us right now, Freedia. This is just the beginning." When I hung up the phone, I dialed my mom. I told her about Gaga.

"They'll be coming to you one day," she said with all the confidence in the world.

* * *

IN MAY OF 2011, we headed to B.O.M.B. Festival, which was an event that mixed major artists like Snoop Dogg and Weezer with up and coming local Hartford artists. We didn't fit either category, so I wasn't sure why we were invited, but I was up for everything that came my way.

When we arrived at the venue, I immediately sensed a different vibe. The place was teeming with white kids in cargo pants and short, spiked haircuts. It occurred to me that this was a rich kids' party college. Until then, we'd performed for the sissy-punk scene, the alternative punk scene, and artist scene. Well-to-do fraternity boys weren't exactly our target audience.

"You see this place?" I asked Rusty, as we made our way to the greenroom. Alercation and Heather Loop, a dancer who drove up from New York to perform, were looking wide-eyed at every turn.

"Crazy scene," Rusty said, putting down his bag and equipment. "But we'll be okay, Freedia. They're going to love you."

Turned out, we were scheduled to go on between Wiz Khalifa and Snoop Dogg. After Khalifa's set, the promoter took the stage. "If you want to know what New Orleans is, you need to know about Big Freedia!" The crowd started clapping and whistling. Rusty was already on stage and broke out the usual "Diva Is a Female Hustler" to warm up the crowd.

As the dancers and I walked onstage, the sea of white boys made my heart start beating fast. As we took our places on stage, the festival suddenly got silent. When I started with "Y'all Get Back Now," I noticed some kids in the way back moving and a

cheer here and there, but the front of the place was still. No one was even nodding their heads.

Then, out of the audience, came "Boo!" I thought I may have misheard, but then the craziest thing happened: Over my mic, I heard a decided "Fuck you!!!" coming from one of the kids in the front. I looked around at Altercation and Heather. They were moving. Then, as I was going into "Almost Famous," some kid threw a water bottle at the stage. I moved in time so it missed me, but I'm like, these kids are not trying to see no queen onstage.

"Fuck you!" I heard from the left side of the stage. But I kept going. These bitches were gonna see this whole show. I heard another "Booooooooo!"

About the fourth song in, suddenly another water bottle was hurled and another followed. The last one almost nailed Altercation in the head. She looked at me and my tiger momma came out. I was livid. Throw shit at me all day long, but my dancers, no. Disgusting.

I always try to take the high road in life and be the facilitator of peace. It's gotten me far in my career, and also as a way of life. I really don't care if people don't like me. My momma gave me an unshakable sense of myself. But, there's a line, and these frat boys were irritating me. I walked up to the edge of the stage and looked in the direction of the guys who threw the bottle and yelled, "Fuck ya momma!" as loud as I could. I spotted a kid booing and looked right at him and said, "And yours too!" The crowd went wild. I could see lots of kids in the back jumping up and down. They started chanting, "Big Freedia!" The crowd had turned and most of the kids were supporting us. We finished that show—every last song.

Afterward, me and Rusty went into town to check out the scene. As we were crossing the street, a car stopped at the stop sign. The window went down and a kid stuck his head out the window. "Big Freedia!" he said from the backseat.

I wasn't sure whether to duck or smile, but before I could decide, he said, "You were awesome!"

A girl in the front passenger seat rolled her window down. "We loved the show! I hope you don't let those douche bags scare you away from Connecticut!"

"Okay," I said, "thank you, honey." As they sped off, I started laughing.

"See," Rusty said. "They love you wherever you go, Freedia."

CHAPTER 27
NEW YORK TIMES

ONE MORNING IN JULY 2011, my phone woke me up. "You see the story?" It was Crystal.

"No," I said, sitting up in bed. I was exhausted from performing the night before. "What story?"

"*New York Times*," Crystal said.

"I'm gonna get it; I'll call you back, hear?" I said, suddenly excited to see it. It was noon and it was already so hot, I thought my phone was gonna melt. Since expanding my sets to an hour, I found it even harder to roll out of bed the next day. I strolled into the bathroom and grabbed a cold washcloth to put over my face, hoping it would calm the puffiness. It didn't, so I grabbed some sweats and slipped on my Adidas. I was too exhausted and excited to bother lacing them. I stopped at two or three stores before I finally found the paper for sale in the lobby of a hotel near the Convention Center. There it was, me and Katey Red in color in the paper's Sunday magazine: "New Orleans's Gender-Bending Rap."

"That's me!" I exclaimed to the guy behind the desk, pointing to the picture. I scooped up the remaining four copies.

"I know," he said, handing me my change. "Congratulations!" I read it from start to finish in the car and then drove straight to my mom's.

"Baby, I'm so proud of you," she said. That was just the beginning. The next day, I had a decorating gig for a birthday party at the Chocolate Bar on Broad Street, near Tulane. As I was unloading bags of balloons and ribbons I had just scored at Hobby Lobby, two white guys jogged past me. "Big Freedia!" one of them yelled out and waved wildly. "We love your article in the *New York Times*!"

"Thank you!" I said, waving back. These two college kids knew who I was! The next day I stopped for gas and this older black woman was coming out of the market.

"Are you Big Freedia?" she asked.

"Why, yes," I said. I was starting to love being recognized.

"I saw you in the paper!" she said, raising her coffee cup as if to salute me. "Make us proud." She got into her car and sped off. For months I couldn't go anywhere without someone telling me they read the article. Truth is, I knew that the *Times* was major, but I did not realize the extent. The story was a huge turning point in my career.

My Windish bookings went through the roof. Before the article, I was doing a few out-of-town shows a month, spot dates in places like Indianapolis and Denver. After the article came out, I was on the road almost every week, hitting Chicago, Brooklyn, San Francisco, Atlanta, Portland. I was starting to understand just how important press was if I was going to grow my career.

Sometime around then, Devon and I decided to make a serious go of our relationship. I had moved into a new house of my own on Warrington Drive in the Eighth Ward and he moved in with me, along with a little white poodle I adopted named Rita. A couple of days before I was leaving for Fuck Yeah Fest, he came home and handed me a little blue velvet box. Inside was the most gorgeous diamond band.

"Will you marry me?" he asked.

"Yes!" I said. Despite our arguments, I was in love with this boy. Truth was, knowing that Ms. V was sick, I was in need of some stability.

Me and Nobby also signed the contracts with Boss right before the Fuck Yeah Fest. Boss had shown that he was down for me by working almost a year without a contract, and I felt it was the right thing to do. Once again, I didn't have a lawyer look it over.

Fuck Yeah Fest was the first gig where me, Boss, and Rusty all went out together, along with the dancers. It went down at Los Angeles State Historic Park, located downtown. Groups on the bill were all electro-indie rock bands I had never heard of: the Rapture, Panda Bear, Dead Man's Bones, Cold Cave, Best Coast.

As usual, Rusty was on the grind. He knew this girl Swoon, and when he told her we were coming out to L.A., she asked us to perform at her birthday party. Rusty said this would be big, in part because Swoon was represented by an art dealer, Jeffrey Deitch.

"Jeffrey brought street art to America!" Rusty was all excited. "Keith Haring, Shepard Fairey, Fischerspooner!"

"Okay, I like it," I said. Those names didn't mean anything to me, but it sounded like something I needed to know.

The day we got to L.A., we rented a car and drove straight to Swoon's party, which was at Deitch's house in the Hollywood Hills. This house was off the chain. The floors had this glowing, hologram effect. The living room had stained-glass windows and enormous framed art pieces hanging on the walls. The outside was even more extravagant: it had a great big swimming pool and the most gorgeous succulents sitting in majestic black planters that were six feet high.

The place was packed with white guys with beards and skinny jeans and white girls in cutoff shorts and ankle boots. We ambled about the house like it was a museum. Rusty pointed to a framed black-and-white print on the wall. "Freedia, do you know how cool this is?" he asked. I just stared at him. "This is a Keith Haring!"

"Wow," I said, knowing I should have been impressed, but I kinda felt like I could have done that picture in my sleep.

"Big Freedia! Rusty!" A cute brunette with a pierced septum yelled out to us. "I'm Swoon!" she said, hugging me hard. "Thanks so much for coming! I'm so excited to see you perform!"

"Thanks for having us," I said.

"Let me introduce you to Jeffrey," she said, and an older white man with round-rimmed glasses came up behind her. "I'm Jeffrey Deitch," he said. He rocked a linen jacket and loafers. He was legit. To me the question was, How was he going to react to me and my dancers pussy-popping in his fancy house? *Trust in Rusty*, I coached myself.

I told Jeffrey he had a beautiful home, and he was quickly shuffled away by an assistant.

"Showtime," Swoon said, pointing to the area where she wanted us to set up. The set was short, but we killed it. We started with "Y'all Get Back Now," moved into "Gin in My System," and ended with "Azz Everywhere." The crowd was small, but hyped. Maybe it shouldn't have at this point, but it amazed me how these kids knew my music. I spied Jeffrey watching and I couldn't tell if he was enjoying it or not, but I knew I was about to find out.

After the show, as I was downing my second bottle of water of the night, Jeffrey Deitch approached me. "The show was spectacular," he said.

"Glad you liked it," I said, a little shocked that he was talking to me. He went on to ask me how long I had been doing my music, and if I had an album. I couldn't believe this man was so interested in Bounce.

"Why don't you and your dancers come to my place for lunch before you go home?" Jeffrey asked.

"Sure!" I said. Jeffrey handed me his card and told us to come by on Monday, which was the day we were headed home. In the cab ride back to the hotel, shit got messy. Fact was, we were working hard and we were like a family fighting and arguing.

"Rusty," Rocky said from the backseat of the taxi, "you're sneaky as fuck."

"Hush," I told Rocky.

"What are you talking about, Rocky?" Rusty scoffed, looking back at Rocky from the front passenger seat.

"You know what I mean, bitch," Rocky said. "I'm gonna kick

your ass." Before I knew it Rocky lunged forward and actually went for Rusty's head with a closed fist.

"Settle your drunk ass down," I said, grabbing her arm before it made it to her target. She kept trying to wrestle herself from my grip. "I can't have this on tour!" I said, finally getting her to settle down. "I'm sending you home first thing tomorrow."

I was so heated when we finally got back to the hotel. Turned out, while I was handling Rocky in the car, Devon was calling me. I had like twenty missed calls from him when we got to the hotel room.

"Where you been?" he moaned when I called him back.

"I had a show, I told you that," I said, growing impatient.

"I've been calling you for hours," he said.

"We had a party and sound check, baby," I said as we rolled up to some hotel near LAX. "Lemme call you back."

We had booked two hotel rooms, one for the guys and one for Altercation and Rocky. I called my weed guy the second we got to our room. Then I filled up the bathtub and called the airlines and booked an early flight home for Rocky. I got into the bath and called Devon to try to calm him down. The next morning as I put her in the cab, Rocky was crying.

"He's sneaky," she kept saying. I felt terrible, but I wasn't gonna have fighting from my team.

EIGHT THOUSAND PEOPLE attended Fuck Yeah Fest that year. I remember seeing this sea of indie, punk, electro-rock kids in the audience. Bounce just seemed worlds away from this, but so far,

Rusty had only opened up doors for me and they seemed to be the right ones. Backstage was something else: No one said a word to us. Mel and I were the only black people in sight. A few guys nodded to us, but otherwise, we were the new kids. We had been outsiders, though. *Please, God*, I thought. *Please let this go okay.*

Before we went on, the lead singer of the group !!! grabbed the mic. "Are you ready for some Sissy Bounce?" he hollered, trying to amp the crowd. It was completely silent. I shot Rusty a concerned look. He smiled back at me. The dude repeated, "I said, are you ready for some Sissy Bounce?!" I heard one or two halfhearted screams. I was about to crawl into a corner when Rusty marched out. Me and the dancers had no choice but to follow.

We started with "Gin in My System." Altercation was moving and shaking. When I called out, "I got that gin in my system," no one responded, so I chanted the call and the response. A funny thing happened, though: by the end of the song, the audience got it. I'd hold out the microphone and got "Somebody's gonna be my victim!" Girls from the audience started to gather at the front of the stage. By "Y'all Get Back Now," girls were really starting to cut it up. When I did "Azz Everywhere," they started to bend over and shake their asses. And the minute the girls get into it, the boys do too, because what straight guy doesn't want to watch girls clap their asses? Standing there, I could see I was winning over the audience.

After our set, the vibe backstage changed. People were high-fiving us, saying how cool they thought the show was. Just as I was finishing a joint, this guy approached me saying he was from Carson Daly's TV show and that he wanted to know if I'd be interested in being on it.

"Of course!" I said. I knew who Carson Daly was from MTV. "When?" We were leaving in two days.

"We'll shoot tomorrow or the next day," he said. "We just need to find a location." He said he'd call us the next day to let me know when and where the shoot would take place. It was one thing to be in the newspaper, but another to be on national TV! I was so excited.

As we were walking to the car, this girl with purple hair and Dr. Martens walked up to us. "Excuse me," she said. "I'd like to speak to you about that song, 'Gin in My System.' The line 'Somebody's gonna be my victim'? That condones rape." She wasn't letting us move past her.

I was too stunned to speak, and suddenly the excitement about Carson Daly disappeared in an instant. Thank God, Rusty didn't skip a beat: "I'm happy to have this conversation with you, but not right now."

"Does Big Freedia condone rape?" she pressed on.

"This is an important discussion," Rusty said, calmly. "But I need to pack up my equipment right now." I think she was surprised that Rusty remained so cool and she walked away, but not without some choice words I won't repeat.

I have to admit, that was the first time I thought about those lyrics in that way. In no way do I condone assault or any violence against women. On the contrary, my fan base is and has always been largely female, because I provide a safe place for women to be free of their inhibitions about their bodies. My message is to shake what you have, whatever size, whatever your sexual preference. *Victim* is simply a term that me and the other sissies used to identify someone we wanted to get with or liked. In my world, that's how we speak.

When we got into the car, I lit up a cigarette. "God," I sighed, scanning the L.A. skyline.

Rusty turned to me. "Don't let it get to you. At some point, people have to understand that Bounce is a culture with its own rules. You're sharing it with those who want to be a part of it for a night."

"Right," I said, as we merged onto the 10 freeway.

"If they don't like it, there are tons of other artists out there," he added. I took what Rusty said that night to heart. At this point, that song is an old standby and a classic at a Big Freedia show. I know 99 percent of the people who come out understand what I mean.

When the day came to shoot Carson Daly, Rusty got a frantic call from the location scout, saying the site they had in mind was suddenly unavailable, and so they were going to have to find a new place.

Rusty took out his phone and dialed. "Hi, Jeffrey, this is Rusty Lazer." Pause. "I wanted to know if we can shoot Big Freedia and Carson Daly at your house tomorrow. They are looking for a location." Pause. Then, "Okay, uh-huh. Great!" Rusty looked at me: "Jeffrey said we could shoot at his house!"

"Amazing!" I said. Rusty called Carson's people back to let them know.

I was nervous as hell that day. This was my first TV appearance. I primped and preened in the bathroom as much as I could. I rocked a plaid button-down and white jeans.

"Let's go," I said to Rusty. We met Altercation at the parking lot and packed into the car. As soon as we arrived, my stomach felt all twisted up. I couldn't believe I was going to meet Carson Daly.

When the crew got there, they started to set up cameras. "Where's Carson?" I asked, excitedly.

"He isn't coming," the camera guy said. "We're gonna have you talk into the camera about Bounce, what it is, its origins, how long you've been doing it."

"He's not coming?" I asked.

"No, we'll cut it together for the show," the cameraman said. "It'll look great!"

"Okay," I said, a bit disappointed not to be meeting him. But as soon as the cameras started to roll, I just ambled around the house and started talking. I saw this grand piano in the living room and walked over to it. I rested on it while I looked into the camera and explained about the origins of Bounce. I felt totally at ease.

"You did great," Jeffrey said as we enjoyed lunch by the pool. It was an amazing day. Looking back now, I'm not mad at Carson at all. Actually, I'm extremely grateful to him, because he was the first national TV show to cover me. And I was starting to understand very clearly that I couldn't put a price on all the people I was meeting through Rusty.

PART OF THE SCION DEAL was a budget for a video. I had never shot a professional one before and I was excited to work with real directors and producers. I decided on the track "Y'all Get Back

Now," because it was a club favorite and it was my newest song at the time. Rusty knew these two directors from a New Orleans–based film company called Court 13, Bob Weisz and Josh Ente. When we met with them, I was feelin' their concept of a *King Kong*–style video where I was larger than life, lumbering around New Orleans twerking and shaking.

We decided to shoot the video on December 21, right before the holidays. I remember like it was yesterday. The TV hummed in the background while I gathered my outfits. I had four wardrobe changes for the day: a white leather studded jacket compliments of Uncle Percy, the purple gingham, red leather jackets, and my all-black backup outfit.

On set, Ms. Tee called my phone and said Magnolia Shorty had been shot and killed in a drive-by shooting. I dropped the jacket I was holding and ran to the TV. My hands were shaking as I turned up the volume. No. No. No, this couldn't be true.

It was. She was in a car with a friend, and they were sprayed with bullets—wrong place and wrong time. I fell to the floor and just started sobbing. This girl who was so special to me. Another killing for no reason. Disgusting.

I called Rusty and told him I couldn't shoot the video.

"Freedia, we have to. We booked everyone. They are ready to go."

Between sobs, I told him I'd be at the location. I knew I had to keep going. I was in a fog all day. I was so filled with raw emotion that I honestly think it came off better than I ever imagined. In the meantime, my Facebook and phone were blowing up with people commenting about Magnolia. She was a beloved figure in our city.

A week later, I attended Shorty's funeral at Fifth African Baptist Church, my momma's church. It was a New Orleans jazz funeral. There was no room inside the church and hundreds, maybe thousands, of people stood outside. Lil Wayne, Mannie Fresh, and Birdman attended. After the casket was brought out and put into a horse-drawn carriage, she was taken away. A second-line band with horns and drums marched all the way to Shakespeare Park. Just another tragic day in New Orleans. But also a celebration of the life of another Bounce artist who will never be forgotten.

CHAPTER 28
RENEE

TWO THOUSAND TEN was a rough year. Between the murders of Magnolia Shorty and Hockey, as well as my mom's cancer, I seriously considered calling it quits. When I told Ms. V I didn't know if I could go on, she wouldn't hear of it. "God got me, Freddie," she always said. "Handle your business."

Turned out, 2011 was just as crucial. I knew Rusty was going to be hot when he found out I signed paperwork with Boss, since he was de facto managing me. That was the beginning of the rift between me and Rusty. I felt like we were both starting to see his role differently. He wanted to be my manager and one half of the "Big Freedia and Rusty Lazer Band." I wanted—have always wanted—to be a solo artist. Plus, I wanted to use other DJs sometimes. A lot of locals, K-Real, DJ Lil Man, and DJ Poppa, had helped get me to where I was and represented Bounce as much as Rusty. I wanted to put them on too.

Devon and I were having serious problems as well. That boy can be the best boyfriend when he wants to be and the most callous fuck I've ever known. He would get distant with me and it would drive me crazy with fear that he was cheating. I'm not sure if I feared it so much that I willed it to happen, or if it was going to happen either way, but one night he just didn't come home. I blew up his phone. When he didn't pick up, I drove to his mom's house and knocked on the door. She came out.

"Where's Devon?" I asked.

"He's not here, Freedia." I drove home and called him a hundred times. He finally showed up at home a few days later.

"Where the fuck have you been?" I asked.

"Nowhere," he said.

"Bitch, I know you're cheating on me." We fussed so long that night I can't even remember how it ended. The next morning, when Devon was in the shower, his phone rang and I decided I was going to see who the fuck was blowing up his spot.

"Who's this?" a girl said on the other end of the line.

"I'm his boyfriend, baby. Who are you?"

"I'm Shannon," she said. "Boyfriend?"

"Yes, honey, your man is gay!" I said.

"Well, I'm having his baby!"

I hung up the phone and swallowed hard. Why would she lie? I needed some smoke. Shit, I felt like I was on an episode of *Maury* fucking *Povich*. When Devon got out of the shower, I got up in his face. I started yelling, "You got a bitch pregnant?!"

Devon didn't even deny it. He had been sleeping with her for months.

"It's hard when you on the road, Freedia," he said.

"Are you in love with her?" I asked, not sure if I really wanted to hear the answer.

"Nah."

"Are you straight?"

Tears welled up in his eyes. "I don't know."

"Who do you love? Men or women, Devon?"

"That's just it," he said. "I can find emotional connection from a woman or a man." And there it is. Trade boys. Sexual culture in New Orleans is a funny thing. But it doesn't matter. Like I said, we make definitions that work for us down here. Devon eventually did leave Shannon, and I still help pay child support, because I don't want to leave that baby hanging.

THAT WAS THE BEGINNING of some very rocky times for us. I remember one night Rusty said, "You are in an open relationship, Freedia." To me, I'm not. For someone whose gender is so fluid, I can be very black and white. I know it sounds crazy, but I want Devon to be with me and me only.

Either way, I couldn't trust him, and his cutting out would make me more suspicious. One night after a show, we were driving home and we got into it again. It was the same fight over and over.

"Fuck you, bitch! I know you're stepping out on me!"

"Fuck you, Freedia! Leave then! I don't give a fuck!" he screamed back. And then something just clicked in me. I swerved the car to the side of the road, next to an old, uninhabited shopping center blocked with barbed wire. I got out, twisted the band off my finger, and threw it over the fence into the rubble. I got back in the car and we rode in silence back to the house.

It continues to be this push-pull that drives me—and my friends who are forced to watch it—to the brink. Love is a crazy thing. I've tried to leave, but something keeps me coming back.

On May 5, 2011, the night before the Queen of Bounce tour, I was packing my bag for Denver when I got this sharp pain in my stomach. I'm not talking a little tummy-ache. I'm talking soreness and nausea, enough so that I had to leave my bag half-packed and curl up in a fetal position on the bed. Devon brought me hot water and made me soup, but nothing would stay down for hours. I was up most of the night feeling like I was going to die. Miraculously, a couple of hours before Boss came for me the next morning, the pain vanished as quickly as it had come. I figured it had to be nerves, with everything happening with my mother, with Rusty, and with my new tour, which would have me traveling all over the Midwest and beyond.

Rusty had suggested his new girlfriend, Corrine, should come on tour and dance. I worried she might throw off the balance of the group, but since I had Devon on the road, I decided to keep quiet for the time being and let her join.

The Larimer Lounge show in Denver went off without a hitch. The next night, in Chicago, we cruised to the Empty Bottle for sound check, and, like always, right back to the hotel to rest. I lit a

smoke on the balcony and instantly my stomach cramps returned, hard. I flipped on the television and lay down for a minute, but it only got worse. After thirty minutes, I was doubled over, sick to my stomach, worse than it had been in New Orleans.

What if I couldn't perform? That could be catastrophic. KT's voice flashed through my mind. "You get one chance to piss off a promoter and they won't book you again."

But I was freaked out about my health too. What if I had stomach cancer? That would kill my momma before her spinal cancer would. And as a gay man, there's always that AIDS fear in the back of your mind. It's not like I had never had unprotected sex. Devon had already admitted to cheating on me once, so who knew what he was up to?

My phone beeped and Boss's name came up. "I need you to come to my room," I said. I managed to unlock my room door before running back to the bathroom. In less than a minute, Boss was standing over me.

"Freedia, you look terrible," he said. "We need to get you to a hospital."

"No, I'll be okay," I said, trying to fight it.

Boss wasn't having it. "Let's go, Free," he said, lifting me off the floor and propping me up against him. In the elevator, Boss called hotel staff and asked for the address of the nearest ER. When we got to the hotel entrance, he sat me down on a bench and told me to wait. Moments later he came around with the van and we flew down the streets of Chicago to the hospital.

By the grace of God, there weren't many people waiting, so I was ushered quickly into a room. As a nurse took my temperature and blood pressure, I tried to stay calm. All I could think about was getting onstage.

"The doctor will be right here," the nurse said, jotting down some notes and shutting the door behind her.

"I'm going to cancel tonight," Boss said.

"No," I said. "We got time."

"You can't go onstage like this, Freedia," he said, shaking his head.

"No, I feel better," I said, and I actually thought I did. But the real reason was that I wanted that money. Just then the doctor appeared. He had me lie down and with his ice-cold hands, he began to palpate my abdomen.

"What is it?" I asked impatiently. The doctor didn't say anything and just kept pressing his fingers and putting his ear to my stomach.

Finally he looked up and removed the stethoscope from his ears. "I don't know," and then he added, "Maybe an ulcer." I was so relieved I wanted to cry. An ulcer? Hell, I didn't even know what that was, but I never heard of anyone dying from one. "You have too much acid in your stomach," he continued, "so I'm going to give you some medicine for it tonight."

He handed me a cup of something. "Drink this," he said. "It'll help with the nausea." As he scribbled out a prescription, he added: "You need to get to a doctor when you get home. They can keep an eye on it and manage it with medication. If you don't do that, you'll have to have surgery."

I felt 100 percent better.

"And get some rest tonight," he said, patting my shoulder.

"Of course," I said, shooting Boss a smile. We stopped by a

Walgreens for the medication and were back to the hotel by eleven thirty. I felt great and it was thirty minutes until showtime.

"Let's get the dancers," I said. We sped to the venue and got backstage with only ten minutes to spare. That night the crowd was feelin' me and I went an extra thirty minutes for them.

I MET RENEE MONCADA, who eventually became my manager, on that tour too. After Chicago we hit Oakland, and after that show we were backstage when this woman walked into the greenroom with natural ringlets framing her caramel face. With her bright red lipstick, she was positively striking.

"I'm Renee," she said.

"You're a beautiful girl," I said. I couldn't stop myself, she was just so gorgeous. I recalled that a few weeks previous, Boss had gotten a call from a woman named Renee who was hyped about doing a documentary on Bounce music. We had gotten all kinds of calls about videos and movies and such, mostly from outsiders who didn't see Bounce beyond ass shaking. Most of the time people talked a big game but didn't come through, so I had learned to proceed with caution.

Renee lived in Oakland, so Boss told her to come to the Oakland show at the New Parish. Ticket sales were sparse, but that didn't mean we didn't go hard as fuck. Another one of KT's mantras: "I don't care if there's one person in the club or five hundred, you perform like it's the last show of your life."

"Nice to meet you," I said, removing my new bedazzled jean jacket and setting my purse on the couch.

"I saw your inspiring story in *BUST* magazine," Renee said. "I want to make a movie!" Turned out, she actually had credentials: she had produced a documentary on the rapper Too $hort and had produced shows for National Geographic Channel and TLC. Her husband is a well-respected producer from the Bay Area who worked with En Vogue and Club Nouveau, so she knew the music business, too.

"Come to New Orleans," I said.

"I will," she said. I liked her well enough, but I'd heard that before. I gave her my number and we walked out onto the street in front of the club.

The van came around the corner and stopped. Before I stepped in I turned around and waved good-bye. "You sure are a beautiful girl," I repeated.

"So are you!" she said.

Driving back to the hotel, I told Boss about her. "I think she's legit." The rest of the tour went off without incident, except I was a little concerned about Rusty's Corrine. I knew Altercation was too sweet to say anything if she felt it, but I never wanted her to feel like she was being pushed out. Altercation had been with me from the start, dealing with all kinds of road-life bullshit, and she'd always have a place on my shake team.

When we returned to New Orleans, I went straight to my mom's. "Hi, Momma," I hollered as I turned the key to the front door. She wasn't in her usual spot in the kitchen or on the couch. The usual aroma of Tony Chachere's seasoning and onion wasn't permeating the house. It was just Uncle Percy alone at the dining table, stitching together some curtains.

"She's in her room," he said softly, without looking up. "That medication's tired her out pretty bad." I hurried into her bedroom, and there she was, propped up in bed, wrapped in blankets, with her arms crossed and her eyes closed. I sat next to her and listened to her slow, careful breath. Her color was a gray I hadn't seen before. And it hit me for the first time: Momma was withering away before my eyes. As I tried to imagine life without her, my eyes welled up with tears. I crawled into bed next to her, and wept as quietly as I could.

She woke up at some point. "Hi, baby! When did you get home?"

"Last night, Momma," I said. "How are you feeling?"

"Oh, I'm doing just fine," she said, and she immediately changed the subject: "How was the tour? That boyfriend being good to you?"

"Yes, Momma."

"He better be," she said. "'Cause I'll whup his ass if he isn't."

I didn't tell her that it just might be a good idea for her to do that.

A COUPLE OF DAYS LATER, I opened the door and there stood Renee, all the way from Oakland, with a camera guy and equipment. For the next seven days, those two shadowed me to Caesar's, to the studio, to Rusty's place, and I even let them meet my mom. Renee got hours of interviews, show footage, and time with Katey Red and Sissy Nobby.

As I got to know Renee, I grew to like her and her vision for the film. A lot of people think Bounce is simply a booty-shaking dance from the ghetto, but Bounce is as shallow or deep as you want to make it. The groin area has extraordinary power. Moving it at lightning speed is more than sexual; it's also deeply intimate and transformative. For us sissies, who lived under such constant oppression—the violence, poverty, and homophobia—Bounce is our way to transmute that pain into joy. Renee understood that. At the end of her trip I was willing to sign a contract, called a talent hold agreement, to give her two years to make a film.

Over the next few months, a shift happened in the team. I know everybody will have a different memory of how it went down, but this is how I recall it: Bojan started to complain that Boss wasn't responding to media requests and was booking local shows on top of out-of-town shows. So Bojan started to go to Renee. I don't know if Bojan preferred her attitude or if she just responded more quickly, but either way, Boss wasn't handling the press requests that were coming fast and furious. Bojan kept insisting, "You need a publicist to get show previews in all the regional papers in the cities you are in."

In June, Renee called me and said she had found a publicist in Beverly Hills: Nicole Balin from Ballin PR. The next show in Los Angeles was in July at the Echoplex, and Nicole came out to meet us. I'm not exactly sure what it was, because we aren't exactly cut from the same cloth—Nikki is a white girl repping Beverly Hills—but there are some people you just click with. She came through with a budget we could work with and was eager to start. I hired her, and to this day, Nicole is a beast.

Beyond finding the right people for the team, Renee was coming up with other fresh ideas. This is when the reality TV show first came into the picture. I want to make it clear that me and Boss had talked about doing a reality show for a while—way before I ever met

Renee. But it's one thing to talk about it and it's another to execute it.

Sometime that summer, Boss got a call from the director Harris Fishman, at a film company called WW7. Harris had some idea about a 3-D documentary with Bounce and booties and butts. Boss directed him to Renee since I had a talent agreement with her. Renee flew to L.A. and met with the director, but ultimately she advised against a 3-D documentary.

"I'm concerned about it trivializing the culture," she said.

"All good," I said.

We didn't hear from the company for a few months, but sometime later that fall, Harris called and said he thought a production company called World of Wonder, which worked on shows like *RuPaul's Drag Race* and La Toya Jackson's *Life with La Toya*, might be interested in a show about me.

At first Renee wasn't feeling the idea of a reality show either. "I'm not sold on the idea. You need to establish yourself as a musical artist first," she said. I was very excited about it, though, so I asked her to meet with them. TV was her world and I was hoping we could use some of her footage to secure something with World of Wonder. After we sent them film, pitches, and story lines, World of Wonder wanted to shoot a sizzle reel they could shop.

In essence, Boss passed the ball to Renee, and she ran with it. Boss's role wasn't ever clear on the TV show, other than representing me as my manager. Renee was starting to go way beyond the role of filmmaker, taking over Rusty's and Mel's managerial roles. The icing on the cake was that she understood fashion. Not only was she glamorous in her own right, but her sister, Leslie, was a makeup artist. I had wanted to experiment with my hair and makeup a bit, and sometimes a queen just has to have a woman's touch. It quickly became obvious that Renee was that woman.

In August 2011, I finally went to see a doctor for my ulcer, at University Hospital. After running some tests, the doctor came into the room and explained to me that the lining in my stomach was breaking down.

"Too much spicy New Orleans food, too much powdered aspirin, and too many cigarettes. We won't do surgery if we don't have to," the doctor said, then sent me home with more medicine.

That same month, Renee came back to New Orleans and we decided to record the video for the song "Nah Who Mad." It helped that her husband had made the original Club Nouveau song called "Why You Treat Me So Bad," so getting the sample rights wasn't a problem. The scene was a Josephine block party, so I invited everyone I knew on Facebook and Twitter to come down and cut it up. Hundreds of people, including tons of kids, showed up and we shot the video in a few hours. Altercation and DJ K-Real were in it, too. To this day, that's one of my favorite videos, as well as a song that has become a staple at my shows.

Sometime that summer, Windish booked me on the Check Yo Ponytail tour. Check Yo Ponytail was started by Franki Chan, this young kid who had spearheaded the new punk scene in L.A. and had apparently seen me at Fuck Yeah Fest. Starting in October, we would hit New York, Chicago, Seattle, and Miami, wrapping up in ten days. Like Fuck Yeah Fest, this was the new creative punk world, with groups like Spank Rock, Death Set, and Pictureplane.

Before we hit the road, I went to the doctor for a routine

checkup on my stomach. I had been seeing him now a couple times, so this was standard procedure. He started to feel around my stomach and then he found the spot that sent me through the roof.

I sat straight up.

His face became gravely serious. "I need to feel that again, Freddie," he said, moving toward my belly once more. It was all I could do to let him probe that area.

"You need surgery," he said.

"I'm about to go on tour for the next month," I said. "How about November?"

He removed his glasses. "Freddie, I mean right now. Today."

"What?"

"The lining of your stomach is making too much acid and the medications aren't managing it. Surgery can't wait," he said. "Is there someone you'd like to call?"

"My mom," I said. While I waited for Ms. V to get to the hospital, they prepared me for surgery. I called Boss and told him.

"They already talkin' you got AIDS," he said. I called Nicole and told her to send out a press release that stated I had admitted myself into surgery for my ulcer. Before my mother even got there, I was put under. That day they removed the part of my stomach that was cooking up the acid.

THANKFULLY, IT ONLY TOOK ME a couple of weeks to fully recover, so I was okay by the Check Yo Ponytail tour in October. When we got to L.A., the show was at the Mayan Theater on a Monday night, typically not a great night for shows. But Nicole said that the booker from *Jimmy Kimmel Live!*, Mac Burrus, was coming. Kimmel would be an opportunity of a lifetime.

When we got to the theater I told the dancers I wanted to meet with them backstage. "We got to kill it!" I told them, projecting confidence. "Rocky, you need to bring it. I don't wanna see your lazy-ass shit out there anymore."

All night, I kept eyeing the open space from backstage, hoping people would fill it out, but they were coming in slowly. I'd say a quarter of the venue was filled by the time it was our turn to go on. Regardless, we went out and tore it up! I think we got the best crowd response that night of any of the bands, but honestly, that's how it was the whole tour. Mac came backstage to meet me and said he loved the show. Now it was up to Nicole to take it to the finish line.

That year ended on a high note. First, I was invited to perform at Fun Fun Fun Fest in Austin, Texas. There were rumors that Ryan Gosling was at the festival, because he was filming a movie—but when I found out he was coming to my show and wanted to meet me, I couldn't believe it. And I didn't, until after my show, when he walked backstage.

"Great show!" he said, holding his hand out and bringing me in for a shoulder pound. I blazed up a blunt and offered it to him. He pointed to my new Sailor Jerry tattoo. "How many you got?"

"Many, honey," I said. I turned around and showed him the dick on my back. That moment was a career highlight.

In December, the "Nah Who Mad" video came out, and it looked fly as fuck! We sent that thing to all the press we could, including Mac at *Kimmel*. A week before Christmas, Nicole called me: "We booked *Kimmel*!"

CHAPTER 29

JIMMY KIMMEL LIVE!

B Y 2012, RENEE WAS MAKING power moves for me. She found me a publicist, a tour manager, and a music lawyer, and was talking to a business manager to help me manage my finances. World of Wonder had finished the sizzle reel for the show—using much of Renee's footage—and started to shop it to the networks like MTV, VH1, Logo, and Fuse.

In the meantime, the *Jimmy Kimmel Live!* performance was set for January 25 and it would change my life. For starters, it was my first network TV appearance. I really wanted to represent New Orleans and make my city proud. Part of what had secured the booking was the video for "Nah Who Mad," and Mac expressed interest in replicating that to a certain degree on TV. That meant Devon, the neighborhood kids, and the overall uptown neighborhood feel was essential.

In addition to "Nah Who Mad," we decided to perform "Excuse!"

It was right around then that I had been thinking about adding male dancers to my show anyway. They have so many dope moves—the Shoulder Hustle, the Peter Pan, the Cross Up, Tap It Up, and Rodeo High Step. Fact was, Devon had killed at Fun Fun Fun Fest, and straight guys were increasingly becoming part of the fan base of my shows, so it was perfect timing to add male dancers.

At the time, the best male dancer in New Orleans was this kid Shelby Skipper, aka Skip, a member of a dance troupe headed up by this local cat, Big Choo. I had known about Skip for years because he was a fixture on the dance scene and I had met him at SXSW a few years back. "Gonna need you really soon," I told him that day in Austin. In early January I called him up and asked him if he wanted to join me on *Kimmel*. He agreed and has been with me ever since.

For the girls, we brought Altercation and Rocky, even though I could tell Altercation's heart wasn't in it anymore. I don't know if she was just tired or if she felt replaced by Corrine, or maybe some of both. For an entirely different reason, I was starting to feel like Rocky needed to go. Her attitude was getting in the way of her dancing and I was tired of it. *Kimmel* would be the last time both of those girls danced for me.

As it turned out, we couldn't use any of the young kids because Budweiser is a sponsor of *Kimmel*, and kids can't appear on TV with alcohol logos. Disappointing them was my only regret in that experience.

When I decided to bring K-Real instead of Rusty to DJ, I realized a major downside of getting bigger was having to hurt people sometimes. I wanted K-Real because he was the DJ in the "Nah Who Mad" video, and I was trying to replicate those visuals. But that decision hurt Rusty deeply. His view was "I've been down with you for so long, putting in all this time, now you've made it to *Kimmel* and you aren't going to let me be on it?" And I get where he's coming from. Truth is, Rusty was part of how I did get on *Kimmel*. But this just underscored how we had different views of our roles. I felt like there were going to be a lot of other opportunities, and I'd get him on the next one. Rusty didn't see it that way, and I know my decision did irreparable damage to our relationship.

I decided to bring my mom, because she was getting sicker and I couldn't bear to be away from her. We spent an entire day prepping for the show. My stylist at the time was Renee's younger sister, Leslie Moncada. She got up at 5 a.m. and waited outside an H&M store in San Francisco to cop me this black-and-white-striped Versace outfit and bring it to L.A.

Renee contacted Frank Gaston, Beyoncé's choreographer, who agreed to meet me and the dancers to rehearse at the Kimmel studios. When we pulled up to the parking lot of the El Capitan building at Hollywood and Highland in L.A., I could feel goose bumps on my arms. This was really happening.

As the door guy checked our names, I felt like, This is it: I've made it, and I was so happy that I had brought my momma with me to share in the moment. After rehearsing for a couple of hours, we headed to the greenroom to wait for the taping. When I spied "Big Freedia" spelled out on a name plate on the dressing room door, I had to stop and snap some photos.

When it came time to tape, Mac had this idea to start me walking down Hollywood Boulevard and make an entrance onto the *Jimmy Kimmel* stage from the street. Mac was the guy standing on the street who I pushed out of my way. Everyone thought that was unplanned, but we had rehearsed it.

Devon and Skip killed it that night, and it was such an honor to meet Jimmy Kimmel. I will always be grateful to Mac for that booking. I know it wasn't easy convincing Jimmy Kimmel that a six-foot-two queen from New Orleans was a good idea to have on his show.

As we left the Kimmel building, I took the name tag with me. Back at the hotel, I could barely sleep. I was a ball of nerves and it was gonna take hours to come down. Good thing the bitches back home got nothing better to do but hate. I started to check out my Facebook and phone. Nobby was saying "that Madea-looking bitch" and others were saying I looked like the zebra from *The Lion King*. Okay, that one was actually funny, but Madea-looking bitch? Nobby can't ever take the high road. Good thing I was so high that night from excitement, my whole body was buzzing. No one could have taken that joy away from me, especially because I was blessed enough to rep my hometown of New Orleans.

CHAPTER 30

DREAMS BECOME REALITY

A COUPLE OF WEEKS AFTER *KIMMEL*, Renee called to tell me that Jeremy Simmons, an executive producer at World of Wonder, said we had a firm offer from Fuse TV—a music network owned by Madison Square Garden (at the time) and based in New York, for the reality show. Fuse is a video station, like MTV was in the nineties, so in a lot of ways it seemed like a good fit. Truth was, all the other networks had passed, so we didn't have a lot of choices.

Renee was now the point person for the TV show, in on creative meetings, leaving Boss's position unclear at best and him totally out of the loop at worst.

Meanwhile, I was getting ready to hit the road for a rigorous fourteen-week tour. A few days before we left, my stomach was aching. I was home one day, and at some point I just started to throw up again. But this time I couldn't stop. I just kept going and going. Devon put cold towels on my forehead. Even my poodle, Rita, knew something was wrong. She just paced the house, whining. As I was lying on the bathroom floor, I suddenly felt the most severe burn in my stomach.

"Call the ambulance," I told Devon. "And my momma." The ambulance came and rushed me to University Hospital. A team of ten doctors performed another surgery on me that day. They removed part of my stomach and some of the lining. All the aspirin and Goody's powder I was taking for my headaches had burned the lining in my stomach. I loved those doctors; they saved my life. They also told me they were fans and had my music going in the background while they performed the operation.

I had to cancel the entire tour. That meant Colorado, Ohio, Texas, Michigan, Indiana, and more. We sent a press release out to my fans to try to control the story, but Boss said that there were still whispers around town that I had AIDS. That was a real scare. I didn't leave New Orleans for another few months.

I think it ended up being better that I was home; there were personal and business relationships that I needed to tend to. For one, Altercation called me one day in March and said she wanted to pursue her singing and was going to move on. She was too gracious of a person to say it was because of Corrine or to complain about the pay. That girl's voice is off the chain and I know she is somewhere recording some beautiful music.

Later that year, Rusty and I severed ties too. The catalyst was when I found out that he was managing another sissy rapper, Nicky da B, Katey's gay daughter and former dancer; Nicky was buzzing off a single she released, "Hot Potato Style." I'm not going to lie, she was dope. And I say "was" because she died last year of unknown causes. She was a lyricist and bringing some interesting electronic elements to her music. Rusty was starting to deejay for Nicky, which was fine. Since I didn't want to be exclusive with him, I couldn't expect him to be exclusive with me. But when I found out that Windish was also repping Nicky da B, I was mad. It was a conflict of interest, and I was hurt that Rusty didn't tell me before hooking up the deal for Nicky.

The thing that sealed the deal for me, though, was when I heard that the producer Diplo, of the label Mad Decent, wanted to work with me and had been trying to reach me. I honestly don't even remember who told me, Renee or Mel or who, but I suddenly heard Nicky da B and Diplo were coming out with a song together, and I was heated. I felt that Rusty probably gave it to Nicky out of revenge.

Everyone has different sides to a story and one thing I've learned in the past few years is I'm not always right. When I confronted Rusty, he said that he had offered Diplo to me on a number of occasions and I didn't respond or seem to care. The truth is, so much was happening then with my career and my momma that he might be right. Rusty and I had our differences, but he was not a liar. Either way, it wasn't my intention to blow off Diplo.

Regardless, at that point I felt like it was a conflict of interest for Rusty to be down with both me and Nicky da B. Also, I had decided to bring on Renee as a full-time manager, so I took it to mean that that was the way God planned it.

In May 2012, I made Renee my manager, and Boss my regional manager. There were a ton of things going on for me in New Orleans, and Mel knew this city like the back of his hand, so it seemed like a good solution. Mel accepted it, but I knew I hadn't heard the end of it.

I also realized soon after that that I didn't want to be with Windish. Them repping Nicky da B was a breach of trust that I couldn't get past. Renee had been talking to other booking agents, including the Agency Group, and she was really excited about what they could do. So in October 2012, Renee and I called Bojan and told him we were going to leave Windish. That phone call was excruciating. Bojan was livid, blaming Renee for causing the rift. The bigger my career gets, the more that's at stake. Bojan and Windish did a lot for my career and helped me in ways I could never repay, but it was time to close that chapter in my life.

That summer, "Express Yourself" came out with Nicky da B and Diplo. It exploded on the Internet, and it was dope. I'm glad Nicky left this world something so beautiful before she passed. That song was meant for her and no one else.

CHAPTER 31
MILEY CYRUS

IT KILLED ME EVERY TIME I had to get on the road and leave my mom, but my career wasn't showing any signs of slowing down, ya heard me? In the spring of 2013, I went on tour with the group the Postal Service, and it created more noise than I ever anticipated. The way it happened was that the lead singer of the band, Ben Gibbard, caught a show of mine in Seattle and loved it, so he advocated for me to open for some of the dates on the group's 2013 reunion tour. I was honored and humbled that a musician on his level would want me.

Before the tour started, the press asked about the indie rock and Bounce lineup, to which Ben went on record saying that was part of the draw. I thought the surprising pairing was cool too.

The thing is, it only made me want to try harder when we went out there.

That was the first tour that I had the new lineup of dancers—the ones who have remained with me now. I had seen this dancer Antionique Price, aka Tootie, who, like Skip, was part of Big Choo's dance squad. She had come to many of my shows at the Republic, and she was a ridiculous shaker. I asked if she wanted to do a few shows with me in Houston and try it out. She's been with me ever since. She had a friend named Steph who could also dance. She pushed for her, so I brought them both with me.

At that point I needed one more male dancer, and that's when Boss found this kid Clarence Allen, aka Flash, with a tricolored Mohawk. Flash came from a more straight hip-hop dance background, but he was something else. He could do the pop-locking, the isolations where it looks like you have dislocated from your body and joints, and the crunking, where you jump up and down. I needed someone for a one-off show in San Francisco, so I flew him out so I could meet him and see what he could do. He showed up that night and killed it. He was in.

Now that Rusty was gone, I needed a new DJ who could come on tour with me. Touring is rough and demanding and I needed a young kid who could pick up and go places and who wasn't afraid to travel. I also needed someone without a police record who could travel overseas. And while this may seem like a no-brainer, where I come from it's not. There were a few times when dancers couldn't travel with us because of their records. As God would have it, one night I was filling up my car with gas when I ran into

this kid I knew named Juan Jordan. A spindly brother with dreads, he deejayed around town.

"You gotta police record?" I asked.

"No," he said, and laughed.

"You wanna come on tour with me?" I asked.

"Um, yes! When?" he asked.

"Day after tomorrow?" He gave me his number, and we brought him on tour and that was a wrap. He's still with me today.

The Postal Service tour was a trip. I didn't think too much of it before it started. In fact, I didn't think anything of it. I was honored that I was asked and always up for something new. What could go wrong? I guess some Postal Service fans weren't too pleased about a Bounce artist as the opening act. The first few shows, the audience remained in their seats. The *Seattle Times* ran the headline "Big Freedia Opens for Postal Service, Bewilders Crowd." The article went on to say: "In the normally neutral space of the the Key Arena, audience members were irritated, seemed uncomfortable with Freedia's brand of sexual expression . . . " Another blog bore the headline "Exceedingly White Postal Service Fans Are Confused by Big Freedia Serving as the Band's Opening Act." It was crazy. My Twitter was blowing up with people hating on me and my dancers.

As I said, that tour was a trip. I can remember some of those venues where people just remained sitting in their seats. Baby, you don't come to a Big Freedia show and not shake! In the end, though, we turned Los Angeles, San Francisco, and a few other spots into Big Freedia fans. I had a blast on that tour and I will always be grateful to Ben Gibbard for giving me the chance to be his opening act.

WHEN I GOT HOME FROM THAT TOUR, my momma's condition had deteriorated. The doctors said she probably had a few more months at most and they suggested putting her in hospice. I drove straight to her house from the airport. I slipped past Uncle Percy, who was asleep on the couch. He had been doing a lot of the heavy lifting with Ms. V while I was gone.

I sat with her on the bed. I carefully draped a blanket over her bald head. As I dropped a dose of morphine under her tongue, I thought how ironic it was that after all those years, when she did everyone else's hair for a living, now she had none herself. Mind-numbing that she was only fifty and about to die. I wasn't ready for my momma to leave me yet, so I went into this state of denial. Somewhere inside me I knew she didn't have long, but I couldn't allow myself to accept it.

ON AUGUST 23, 2013, Miley Cyrus twerked onstage with Robin Thicke at the MTV Video Music Awards. This fucked up the music industry for damn near a month. It's all anyone was talking about, and it led people to wonder about the origins of this dance move. The obsession with booty shaking had been growing, but Miley made twerking mainstream. It became an entry in *Merriam-Webster's* dictionary and now is a term every suburban mom knows.

The media went crazy over it, and it generated a lot of press for me. I went on National Public Radio, *Totally Biased with W. Kamau Bell*, *Watch What Happens Live*, HuffPost Live, BuzzFeed, and a slew of other outlets that wanted to know about the origins of this phenomenon that we'd been involved in at block parties since I was in diapers.

Of course, everyone wanted to know where I stood on the appropriation of black culture, and like I said, I don't like to get too heady with these things. I know others can see it from that standpoint, and I prefer to leave it to them to break it down. That said, I want our culture to be credited. It's a sensitive topic since so much black culture has been exploited by the dominant culture. I really appreciate the writers who came to me for some context and background on Bounce. Regardless, it was an amazing boost for me at the perfect time, right before season one of my show, and so I can't thank Miley enough. And the offer still stands for twerking lessons, baby.

In the meantime, the show was getting ready to debut on Fuse in October. The Fuse PR team came up with the idea to attempt to set the Guinness World Record for most people twerking at once. We did it in September, hoping the stunt would get attention for the show's premiere in October.

It worked. We headed out that morning to New York's Herald Square and barricaded a couple street blocks. Fuse had done lots of promotions leading up to the event, so hundreds of people showed up. The only rules were we had to twerk for at least two minutes without stopping to set the record with the Guinness records official presiding. People from all ages, races, and sexualities came out to support us, including a seventy-two-year-old woman named Joan who shook her ass off.

One thing I'm so grateful for is that Fuse paid for me to bring Ms. V. She was so weak by then and it meant the world for me to have her close. The thing was, at every turn my career was growing, and all the while I was watching my momma fade. Amazing how life is like that. They were the most joyful and the most heart-wrenching times of my life.

In the meantime, when Renee got a producer credit on the TV show and Boss didn't, Boss was furious. We worked it out, but not without some ugly words thrown around. They have very different styles and visions, and sometimes I get confused myself. Truth is, sometimes the discord between them is unbearable. Like my momma said, it's show business, baby, and the show must go on, so I try to take it in stride.

Season one aired on Fuse in October 2013. The best part about it was that Ms. V was a huge hit and we had so much fun filming it. The season consisted of six episodes and when ratings came out, it was Fuse TV's highest-rated original series in its history.

I'd like to think that it's at least in part because the series shows many different sides of black life. I don't want to hate on anyone else, but too many reality shows on TV today portray black women as unstable, weave-snatching gold diggers. I'm proud that my show depicts the many sides of black and gay life and I'm thankful to the producers of the show for sharing my vision.

CHAPTER 32

THE ORIGINAL QUEEN DIVA

I HAD A SHOW IN PORTLAND, OREGON, on April 1, 2014, for Red Bull at Mississippi Studios. Portland is crazy. The last time I had been there was in July 2013, when I was on tour with the Postal Service. Someone from the audience yelled, "Get off the fucking stage!" I love my Portland fans, but seems like there's a voodoo spell over that place or something.

Mostly I was on the fence about leaving my mom. I told Renee that I had a bad feeling. "Get on the plane, Freedia," she said. "You gotta show." She was right. Missing a show costs money, and I had a lot of people—dancers, family, and my momma—counting on me to pull in a certain amount of cash every month.

I packed my bag and went to my mom's house to say good-bye.

I sat with her on her bed, rubbing her arms. She had her oxygen tank at her side.

"When will you be back?" she asked. She had gotten to the point where she only wanted me to care for her, not anyone else.

"A few days, Momma," I said as my cell phone beeped. It was Boss, calling to tell me he was outside. I switched off the light in my mom's room and gave her a kiss.

"Go on with your life, child," she said, like always. But then something came out of her mouth that I had never heard before: "I won't be here when you get back."

"Hold on, now," I responded, swallowing hard. "Hold on till I get back."

As we rode to the airport, the dancers—Tootie, Re Re, Skip, Flash, and DJ Juan—were crammed in the backseat, doing what they always do: tweeting, texting, and trash talking. The smell of McDonald's was making me feel like I might throw up all over the passenger seat.

"You okay, Freedia?" asked Boss.

"I'm fine, Boss," I said, lighting up a cigarette, hoping it might help settle my nerves.

"Got the right clothes for the show tonight?" I yelled back to the dancers, irritated at the racket. Every one of them needs a mom, and normally I'm up for the task, but that day, I was in no mood. On a good day, one of them is always showin' up in all yellow when everyone else is in blue. On a bad day, they get sent to jail for some stupid shit, like weed possession, or they miss a flight on tour.

"Yes, Mom," Tootie said. "Me and Re Re got red and black."

"We got red and black, boss," Skip answered for the boys. Planning shows is no joke. I have to color-coordinate the dancers, choose the songs, lighting—it takes a hell of a lot of time. As I reach the next stage of my career, the preparation only gets more elaborate. These aren't "twerk-offs" I'm putting on. These are highly choreographed and stylized performances.

The minute the plane touched down in Portland, I checked my phone. I had no new messages. Now I was terrified. Between my family, friends, my team, and random fans who managed to get my number, my phone was always—I mean *always*—ringing, beeping, or chirping in some kinda way.

We all got into the rental car and headed to sound check, which went off without a hitch. Riding back to the hotel to get some rest, my phone finally rang. It was Uncle Percy, who lived with my mom, so I picked up right way. It was my seven-year-old niece, CeCe, on the line. "Me-Me stopped breathing," she said. Me-Me was the name she called my mom.

"Where is Uncle Percy, CeCe?" I asked, hoping maybe she got it wrong.

"Uncle Percy said she took her last breath," she said again.

My hand was shaking. Tootie stopped talking smack for a minute and then the rest of the dancers got quiet. "What's wrong?" she asked.

Just then my sister, Crystal, beeped in on the other line, so I told CeCe I would call her back. Crystal was just cryin'. Then my boyfriend, Devon, called on the other line and before I knew it, my phone was blowin' up.

The next few hours were a haze. I asked Devon and his mother to go to my mom's house and take care of my family until I got home. Somehow I managed to dial Leah, my tour manager. If there's one thing Leah can do, it's fix a problem—and fast. I feel bad because I couldn't even speak when I called, but she knew what happened right away. I needed to get back to New Orleans as soon as possible.

It took about an hour but Leah called the promoters, canceled the show, and got me booked on a plane home. It was a red-eye from Portland to L.A. to D.C. to New Orleans and cost a ridiculous amount of money, but at that point I didn't care. I told the dancers to stay for their scheduled flights the following day, except Tootie. She is my main girl, my daughter, and I needed a female with me. I know the boys love me in their own way, but it's different with them. I just cried and cried the whole flight home, and Tootie held my hand the whole way.

When we landed the next morning, Tootie's boyfriend picked her up. Boss was waiting for me at the terminal at curbside. When I saw him, we both burst into tears. Two grown men standing at the United terminal sobbing. Boss loved my mom too. She had that effect on people.

By the time we rode to my mom's house, it was ten in the morning and the whole family was there: Crystal, CeCe, Adam, Devon, Uncle Percy, my mom's brothers—Clarence Jr., Howard Sr., Cedric Mason Sr., Danny—my aunt, Addie, and Katey Red.

The mood was somber. I just hugged everyone and then slipped outside with Devon for a smoke. I had been dreading this moment for so long. All I wanted to do was curl up in a ball and go to bed, but I was the oldest and I had the most important task of my life in front of me: to bury my mom.

Not, O Gentle Savior," one of my mom's favorite songs. The pallbearers brought my momma's body outside and slipped it into a white carriage covered in purple flowers and purple drapes, pulled by two majestic white horses. The band and Mardi Gras Indians were at attention. The trumpets and horns came from the right; the tubas and drums sounded from the left. Everyone gathered in the street, including the five limousines and the limo bus, and started to move uptown. Honey, we cut it up for my momma! I glanced back and saw my friends, my team, and neighborhood friends among a sea of white and purple clothing and parasols. Police escorts on motorbikes followed close behind. A few cars just pulled over on the side to watch. I remember that a kid—who happened to be biking by—just joined in the procession. It was a funeral fit for a queen and I knew I did my mom right.

When we got to the cemetery with my family, there was an open space in the mausoleum wall that they were going to put my mom in. As Pastor Sanders spoke the last words, I felt dread at laying my mom to rest one final time. He threw flowers on the casket, and prayed for us.

"Ashes to ashes, dust to dust," he said, and everyone walked out. I started to walk out but then I stopped. I couldn't walk away. Devon had to come back and hold me up. I just cried and cried.

After I got back in the limo, we rode away in silence. My life would never be the same.

"Go out there and tell 'em who you are," I heard my momma say. "I have lived my life, now you have to live yours."

"I could kick myself for not being here when she passed," I said as I lit up a cigarette.

"How was you supposed to know?" Devon said. "She wanted you to keep going." My relationship with Devon is filled with stupid drama. And I mean crazy stupid drama. But when Ms. V passed, that boy was there for me. Didn't take long for him to act up again, but for the next twelve days, until the funeral, he was an angel, and I don't know if I could have gotten through it without him.

The first thing I did the next day was go to the funeral home, where she was being prepared for the showing. When they wheeled Momma out on the gurney, my heart was pounding so hard I thought it might come out of my chest. She looked so peaceful covered in a white sheet. I swear she was smiling too. Suddenly, watching her, my anxiety turned into a huge sense of relief. She wasn't hurting anymore—and I wasn't being selfish wanting her to live in all that agony.

When I got home, I went into planning mode. If you aren't from New Orleans, you might not know what a jazz funeral is, but that's how we do it here. We got jazz parades and jazz funerals. That means a main-line band, or marching band, with trumpets and horns, and a second-line band to follow behind and bring up the back. It means Mardi Gras Indians and a horse and buggy to carry the family. All typical New Orleans style. It's as much about grieving as it is about celebration of life. We do it up, and this was going to be extra over-the-top. I got with the insurance company and the mausoleum. The next night, I called all my family together at the house so we could write the program. The whole week leading up to the funeral was spent with my family, cooking, collecting photos, and talking about my mom.

One night as I was busy ordering flowers, Ben Hurvitz, the runner at the time for World of Wonder, called and asked if they could film the funeral for season two. I had to think about that one. My fans had really loved my mom. She damn near stole the show from me in season one. But I was not about to have anyone use the occasion for TV ratings or anything like that. First thing I did was ask Crystal and Adam. They both were okay with it, as long as it was tasteful. I prayed on it and decided that as long as the church service and casket were not shown, it was okay. I wanted to let the world celebrate her life too.

All the planning kept me busy and focused for the ten days leading up to the funeral. Decorating is one of my releases. I can get through anything if I'm creating. Since Ms. V's favorite color was purple, I decided on the white-and-purple theme. I ordered hundreds of purple and white flowers for corsages and asked all my family and friends to wear purple and white. I bought my mom a silk shirt and pants, and a gorgeous white jacket. I found some lavender appliqué for my uncle Percy, so he could stitch it on her jacket to make it a one-of-a-kind creation.

The casket flower spread took almost all day long, but damn if I didn't make that thing perfection right there. We ordered hydrangeas, lilies, orchards, mums, daisies, and roses, and I arranged each flower one by one just on the casket.

The funeral was April 12 at Fifth African Baptist Church and it was filled to the rafters. Everyone showed up: my family, dancers, managers, our church members, the World of Wonder staff, and all my friends. We expected six hundred but there were damn near over a thousand people. Standing room only.

Me, Devon, my sister and CeCe, my brother, and my stepdad sat together in the front row. Pastor Sanders, who my mom knew her whole adult life, officiated. My cousin Betty was the mistress of services and summoned everyone up to read poems and sing. When my cousin Gail said how much Momma had helped her through hard times, I could feel all the grief, sorrow, and pain that I had been keeping down suddenly rush through me.

I tried to hold it together. I was gripping Devon's hand so hard, I thought I might actually be hurting him. If I was, he didn't say a thing. He just let me hang on. Just when I thought I might break, my old choir group stood up and fanned out in line behind the pulpit. I was going to lead them, something I hadn't done regularly since I was in my early twenties. Singing in the church choir was how I discovered my love for music, and directing is an extension of what I do now. As I walked behind the pulpit, I locked eyes with Addie. When he smiled, I knew I could do it.

All the conducting hand signals came back to me right away when we started "Come Thou Almighty King." As the sopranos, altos, and tenors crescendoed together, a calm washed over me. The same type of peace that came over me as a little gay boy in the choir and that comes over me when I'm onstage now. It heals the pain and grief of poverty, struggle, losing friends and family, abandonment by my dad, hurricanes, and now the hardest loss of all: my mom. It was somewhere in around the third song that I lost my composure and started to cry. The choir continued, and I felt everyone's love in the church holding me up, and I was able to join in again for the last song, "Can't Nobody Do Me Like Jesus."

As everyone filed out of church, the organist played "Pass Me

BIG FREEDIA'S GUIDE TO BOUNCING LIKE A PRO

Y OU'VE READ MY STORY, now you wanna shake somethin' the next time you're at the club? Here are ten trademark Bounce moves that will have you poppin' it—Big Freedia style!

BUST OPEN:
Put your hands on the wall
and shake yo ass in the air.

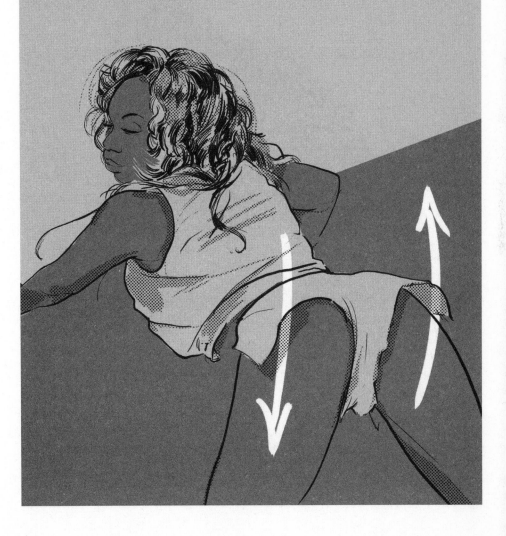

LIFT DAT LEG UP:
One leg on the ground,
        one leg in the air,
and shake it like you just don't care.

THE TWERK:

Squat halfway to the ground
with your legs bent.
Put your hands on your knees
and arch your back.
Then, pop that booty
at lightning speed!

EXERCISE:
Wiggle or swing your hips
from side to side
and keep those thighs
lookin' damn fly.

BOOTY CLAP:

One of the most advanced moves, this entails clapping your ass cheeks like a water wave—shake it fast!

HANDS ON THE WALL:
Squat down
and put your hands on the wall.
Work it and twerk it, baby!

KICK OUT:
Choose a foot, kick it forward like you're trying to get a rock out of your shoe, and then move your body forward, backward, and side to side.

PETER PAN:

First sway your legs and hips in and out, like the old Funky Chicken. When all your lower extremeties are moving, you're doing the Peter Pan!

SHOULDER HUSTLE:
Roll your shoulder up and down,
back to front, side to side . . .
let the music move ya!

ACKNOWLEDGMENTS

FROM BIG FREEDIA:

First, I'd like to thank God, who made all this possible. Thank you to my co-writer, Nicole Balin, for helping me tell my story. Thank you to all of my family who made me who I am today: Crystal, CeCe, Adam, Uncle Percy, Donald Johnson, Freddie Ross Sr., Karen Ross, Clarence Jr., Howard, Cedric, Dawn, Allison, Darya, Janisha, Genitra, Cardell, George, Jaren, Jay, Darnique, Lil Cedric, Linda, Tommique, Lesha, Lil Howard, Trisha, Nefy, Tamara, Christopher, Aunt Lil Debra, Cousin Paula Hart, Cousin Betty Grover, and all my family in Reserve and LaPlace, the Johnson and Hurst families.

Thank you to my gay mom, Mark Bazile, and my dear friend

Craig Adams. Thank you to my other family: Adolph Briggs, Kim and P-Nut, Katey Red, Desmond, and Monney Mone. Thank you to all my Pressing Onward Family Baptist Church family for giving me the unconditional love when I needed it most: Georgia Modica and Remel Burns, Hellene Piper, Richard Stewart, Veronica Dorsey, Clyde Lawrence, Norman Sheppard, Devel Crawford, and my whole Gospel Soul Children family.

Thank you to my team, who keeps me moving forward: Melvin Foley, Renee Moncada, Leah Selvidge, Tim Kappel, Berto Lucci, and Rob Collins. To the baddest crew of shakers on the planet, thank you: Tootie, Re Re, Skip, Flash, Tamika and Diamond, Phat, Steph, Rocky, and my DJ Juan. Thank you to BlaqNmilD, Blaza, J-Dawg, and Law for all the beats over the years. Thanks to the folks and crew at WoW: Chris McKim, John Guevara, Ronnie Hysten, Randy Barbato, Fenton Bailey, and Michael Dugan and the Fuse TV staff. Thanks to the Agency Group and Windish. Thanks to my glam squad, Torelle, Tremelda, Rhonda, Tekoa, Laetitia, and Jessica for always keeping my face made and my hair laid. Thanks to Koury Angelo for the cover and Mike at Mike's Tuxedos for the (last-minute) suit.

Other people along the way who are a key part of my story: Rusty Lazer, Altercation, Corrine, Kenneth Taylor (RIP), Steve Rudison at Money Rules, Gail Sherman, Sissy Nobby, Nicky da B (RIP), Magnolia Shorty (RIP), Ms. Tee, Cheeky Blakk, all my teachers at Walter L. Cohen and Carter G. Woodson. DJs: Lil Man, Poppa, K Real, Tee, all the ones around the world who bump my music. Q93 in NOLA, for always showing love. Mike

Willis and Mr. Adam from Ceasar's, Sims and Twin (RIP) from Sam's. NuNu from Streamline, Cornell from Focus, Miss Vergee and Mr. Gene from Club Escape, and all the others promoters who supported me. A special thanks to promoter Derrick from Unlimited. And last but not least, all my NOLA hood dancers, shakers, twerkers, and pussy poppers from the 3rd to the 17th wards—never stop shaking!

Thanks to Marc Gerald and Jeremie Ruby-Strauss at Simon & Schuster for welcoming me into the publishing world. And thanks to the book whisperer, Rita Williams (Ms. Rita!).

Thank you to my babies, Rita, Sensation, and Royal, for keeping me sane, and last but not least, to the man who keeps me on my toes—for better and worse—my other half, Devon Hurst!

FROM NICOLE BALIN:

First, this book is dedicated to my father, who taught me to appreciate worlds so different from my own.

Thank you to Big Freedia for entrusting me to be the interpreter of this awe-inspiring story. My hope is that you someday truly understand the gift you have for this world. This book would not exist without my endlessly intuitive, supremely gifted writing mom, Rita Williams. Also, thank you to Renee Moncada, Tim Kappel, Ian O'Phelan, Andrew Krents (see, I could do it!), Jennifer Belle, Leah Selvidge, Charlotte Gusay, and Anne Stockwell. You all made this happen in some small or large way. Thanks to Adolph Briggs, Katey Red, Freddie Ross Sr. and Karen Ross, Melvin Foley, and Rusty

ACKNOWLEDGMENTS

Lazer, for the generosity with your time in explaining your stories. Thank you to our editor, Jeremie Ruby-Strauss, and thanks especially to editorial assistant Nina Cordes at Simon & Schuster for your patience and expertise in taking me through this process.

Finally, thank you to those who always encourage me (and remind me of the humor in all things): Moira Kimball, Rob Kimball, Amy Mautz, Liz Vaughan, Arlene Balin, Greta Kroeker, Karl Larson, Zumbi, Ben Bodipo-Memba, Omar Burgess, Afeez Tijani, Trevor Seamon, Harrison James, Scott Fletcher, Rob Collins, Anna David, and Matt Wechsler. The writing of this book would have been much less enjoyable without you all.

A very special thanks to Shelby Skipper, aka Skip, for your time explaining the Shoulder Hustle, the Peter Pan, and the Kick Out.